P9-DEC-738

THE SOUNDS OF ENGLISH AND ITALIAN

CONTRASTIVE STRUCTURE SERIES

Charles A. Ferguson

General Editor

THE SOUNDS OF

Frederick B. Agard
and
Robert J. Di Pietro

THE UNIVERSITY OF CHICAGO PRESS
CHICAGO AND LONDON

This work was developed pursuant to a contract between the United States Office of Education and the Center for Applied Linguistics of the Modern Language Association, and is published with permission of the United States Office of Education.

Library of Congress Catalog Card Number 65-25118

The University of Chicago Press, Chicago 60637
The University of Chicago Press, Ltd., London W.C.1

Second Impression 1969. Printed in the United States of America

GENERAL INTRODUCTION TO THE SERIES

This study is part of a series of contrastive structure studies which describe the similarities and differences between English and each of the five foreign languages most commonly taught in the United States: French, German, Italian, Russian, and Spanish. Each of the five languages is represented by two volumes in the series, one on the sound systems and the other on the grammatical systems of English and the language in question. The volumes on sounds make some claim to completeness within the limits appropriate to these studies; the volumes on grammar, however, treat only selected topics, since complete coverage would be beyond the scope of the series. The studies are intended to make available for the language teacher, textbook writer, or other interested reader a body of information which descriptive linguists have derived from their contrastive analyses of English and the other languages.

The Center for Applied Linguistics, in undertaking this series of studies, has acted on the conviction held by many linguists and specialists in language teaching that one of the major problems in the learning of a second language is the interference caused by the structural differences between the native language of the learner and the second language. A natural consequence of this conviction is the belief that a careful contrastive analysis of the two languages offers an excellent basis for the preparation of instructional materials, the planning of courses, and the development of actual classroom techniques.

The project got under way in the summer of 1959. The primary responsibility for the various parts of the project fell to specialists of demonstrated competence in linguistics having a strong interest in the application of linguistics to practical problems of language teaching. Wherever possible, a recognized senior scholar specializing in the foreign language was selected either as a consultant or as an author.

Since it did not seem likely that the users of the series would generally read all five studies, considerable duplication was permitted in the material presented. Also, although a general framework was suggested for the studies and some attempt was made to achieve a uniformity of procedure by consultation among those working on the project, each team was given free rein to follow its own approach. As a result, the parts of the series vary in style, terminology, notation, and in the relative emphasis given to different aspects of the analysis.

Some differences in these studies are also due to the wide range of variation in American English, especially in the pronunciation of vowels. No special consideration was given to English spoken outside America since the studies were primarily intended for language teachers and textbook writers in this country. There are also differences in the studies which depend on the structure of each of the foreign languages under comparison. Thus, if a fact of English agrees well with a feature of Italian it may merit little mention, if any, in an English-Italian contrastive study, but if the same fact differs in a complicated and highly significant way from a corresponding feature of Spanish, it may require elaborate treatment in an English-Spanish study.

In the course of the project several by-products were produced, two of which are worth noting as of possible interest to readers of volumes in this series. One, Lingui tic Reading Lists for Teachers of Modern Languages (Washington, D. C., 1962), was compiled chiefly by linguists working on the project and contains a carefully selected and annc tated list of works which linguists would recommend to the teacher of French, German, Italian, Russian, or Spanish. The other, W. W. Gage's Contrastive Studies in Linguistics (Washington, D. C., 1961) consists of an unannotated listing of all contrastive studies whic had come to the attention of the Center by the summer of 1961.

Although the value of contrastive analysis has been recognized for some time, relatively few substantial studies have been published. In a sense then this series represents a pioneering venture in the field of applied linguistics and, as with all such ventures, some of the material may eventually turn out to be of little value and some of the methods used may turn out to be inadequate. The authors and editor are fully convinced of the valu of the studies, however, and hope that the series will represent an important step in the application of linguistic procedures to language problems. They are also agreed in their expectation that, while in another ten years this series may seem primitive and unsatisfactory, the principles of contrastive analysis will be more widely recognized and appreciated.

Charles A. Ferguson
Director, Center for Applied Linguistics

TABLE OF CONTENTS

INTRODUCTION 1

1.0.

The purpose of this study is to present a systematic comparison of the Italian and English languages. It is a study based on the findings of linguistic science, but it is not addressed to linguistic scientists. It is addressed rather to those persons, mainly teachers and textbook writers, who are concerned in a professional way with the teaching of Italian to students whose native tongue is English.

There is no implication that the truth about Italian and English is here revealed for the first time, or that the facts of any language can be ascertained only through the study of linguistics. Unified scientific inquiry into the nature of language is only about a hundred and fifty years old, but for centuries scholars have applied rigorous methods to the analysis of languages. Panini wrote his grammar of Sanskrit more than two thousand years ago; it still ranks as an exellent model of linguistic description. The grammarian who revised the Greek alphabet to fit Latin did a formidable job. As a more recent work, Buck's Latin Grammar stands as monumental. For the modern languages, any number of texts furnish wholly accurate and useful information. In the field of language pedagogy, a great variety of effective techniques are in use by experienced teachers who have never formally studied linguistics.

We have therefore no thought of suggesting that the established language teacher should abandon his great storehouse of experience, gained perhaps through the long and laborious trial-and-error application of traditional principles. We would simply offer, to the novice and the seasoned professional alike, the fruits of a systematic study undertaken within the discipline of linguistic science. We have no doubt that the experienced reader will find many of our statements very familiar indeed. We hope he will at the same time encounter much that is new and stimulating. For although the realities of Italian and English exist quite apart from any man's description of them, linguistic science does offer methods and techniques for arriving at accurate insights and for delineating learning problems not always evident in more eclectic approaches.

1.1. WHY A CONTRASTIVE STUDY?

The reader may well wish to inquire whether a systematic study of Italian alone is not sufficient to meet the needs of the teacher or the textbook writer. Why must we bring in English, which we and our students all know anyway? It is not because "Our students do not know English grammar, and must be taught it along with Italian grammar. It is rather because of an important feature of the language-learning process: the student reacts to the learning of a new language largely in terms of behavior patterns imposed by his own language. In other words, he sees the structure of the foreign language through the filter of his in-built native habits; and whether or not he "knows grammar," he is led to commit errors chiefly in those areas where the two languages are structured differently. All languages do differ, and no two in precisely the same areas. Italian contrasts with, say, French in different ways than with English. A contrastive study of Italian and French shows no need to emphasize the existence of two genders: both languages have them, and the grammar of them is exactly parallel. In the contrasting of Italian with English, on the other hand, grammatical gender stands out importantly because Italian has it and English does not. In short, a separate contrastive study for any two languages is necessary in order to identify the learner's problems and to place the emphases where they must go.

In addition, many practical and immediate applications of contrastive analysis are to be found. Robert Lado, in his Linguistics Across Cultures, has this to say about its value (p. 2): "In practice a teacher may be called upon to apply this knowledge under various circumstances. He may be asked to evaluate materials before they are adopted for use. He may be asked to prepare new materials. He may have to supplement the textbook assigned to the class. And he will at all times need to diagnose accurately the difficulties his pupils have in learning each pattern."

1.2. GENERAL VIEWS OF LANGUAGE DESIGN

Several aspects of the design of language as a cultural instrument shared by all human beings have bearing on a contrastive analysis. Among them are the following.

All languages operate with sets of distinctive units recurring in distinctive patterns. Some grammatical units, such as the WORD, are well known to the layman. Other types of unit, such as the PHONEME, are not yet generally recognized or understood.

Patterns are distinguishable in separate and mutually independent layers. Paralleling its grammatical patterns, every language has PHONOLOGICAL patterns— that is, patterns of sound. The basic unit of sound in language design is called the PHONEME; it is more fully defined in Chapter 2.

All languages have a degree of REDUNDANCY. This means that not every unit uttered in a given stretch of speech is absolutely necessary for communication. Normally, no one who understands a language well has to listen to every signal. For example Jack, in order to understand that Jill said, The apples are good, and not The apple is good, did not have to listen for both the -s on apples and the plural verb form are; either alone sufficed him. Yet this was precisely because English grammar obliged Jill to supply both signals; she was not at liberty to eliminate the redundancy and say, The apples is good, or The apple are good.

All languages are, or seem to be, illogical at some points. The patterns of a language have a consistency within themselves, but it is not a consistency equatable with any sort of absolute logic. For example, Italian Non ho visto nessuno may strike the English speaker as logically incorrect, or of saying in effect, I saw somebody, because of the double negative which according to mathematical logic makes a positive. Yet the only grammatical form for that Italian expression contains the two negative words. At one time in the history of English, constructions of the type I didn't see nobody were grammatical also (e.g., in the speech of Chaucer). Perhaps a vestige of this "complete" negation is the modern English use of neither . . . nor as the negative counterpart of either . . . or.

Languages are constantly changing, reshaping their structure, shifting their patterns. Although day-by-day changes in the web of language are imperceptible, striking differences often become obvious after a few short years. The present study takes account of this constant evolution, describing each language as it actually is in the mid-twentieth century, not prescribing it as it once was in the minds of grammarians long gone.

1.3. LANGUAGE AND WRITING

It is important to realize that language and writing are not the same thing. The writing of a language is a reflection of that language and not the language itself. Language is as old as man. Writing is a comparatively recent invention— indeed, there are innumerable persons today who can neither read nor write. Our contrastive analysis is of the Italian and English languages, not of their respective writing systems. We would be saying essentially the same things if our two languages had no written traditions. For some of our readers, this principle may involve some change in orientation. Awareness of the distinction between language and writing is, however, absolutely indispensable for an understanding of phonology, especially English phonology. In many ways English spelling is a reflection of English phonology as it was centuries ago.

1.4. LANGUAGE AND STYLE

In the minds of many persons, speaking a language correctly is confused with speaking it effectively or writing it elegantly. The major task of the English teacher in an English-speaking society is not to teach his students how to speak the language, which they already knew how to do when they entered school; it is rather to develop their style—that is, to train them to express themselves, in speech and above all in writing, in conformity with the standards of excellence set and imposed by the community. This is not at all the responsibility of the foreign-language teacher, whose students do not have the same kind of problems. Their immediate concern is with learning to speak the language, beginning with the very fundamentals. For them, preoccupation with style must come much later. The inclusion of remarks on style in an elementary text is therefore completely irrelevant, and may even interfere with the students' efforts to master the phonology and the basic grammar of the language.

1.5. DIALECTS AND STANDARD ITALIAN

The widely divergent dialects of Italy—Piedmontese, Lombard, Tuscan, Neapolitan, Sicilian, and so on—have been the center of much discussion and controversy ever since Dante's remarks about them in his *De Vulgare Eloquentia*. Many of the dialects have a strong literary tradition of their own, and a long history of competition in laying the basis for the ultimate standard language. Today the famous *questione della lingua* is resolved: there is one standard, based mainly on, though by no means identical to, the dialect of Tuscany. This standard Italian is spoken to a great extent throughout the mainland, Sicily, and Sardinia, and is rapidly expanding through increased education and improved communications. The original dialects are tending to die out, though not without leaving many sorts of regional traces in the pronunciation and vocabulary of the standard language. At present there are three groups of speakers: those who speak only a dialect, those who command the standard language but also actively use a dialect, and those who speak only standard Italian. The now small number of speakers that make up the first group are almost exclusively elderly and non-urban. There are still a great many speakers in the second group, particularly in the North, but they are steadily decreasing in favor of the third group, which is by far the largest and which contains, significantly, almost all the youth of Italy.

1.6. DIALECT DIVERGENCIES IN ENGLISH

Dialect divergencies are not restricted to Italian; English too has its many varieties. If we scan the entire English-speaking world, we find differences about as sharp as those between the dialects of Italian. Highland Scots, London Cockney, and some varieties of Southeastern American, for example, are all but mutually unintelligible. Within the continental United States alone, however, dialects can hardly be said to exist in the sense that they do in Italy or in the British Isles. There are merely regional varieties of American English, more or less on a par with the regional varieties of standard Italian.

A difference of great importance between Italian and American culture is that of social attitudes toward regionalism in speech. In Italy, Tuscan has from the beginning enjoyed high prestige as a model of "good" or "proper" speech, but in the United States no one area is widely recognized as speaking a "better" English than another. South British "received standard," often referred to more colorfully as "the King's English," is regarded by many as a social asset in the United Kingdom, where there are true dialects and strongly colored regional accents; but in the rest of the English-speaking world, including North America, any English spoken by the educated is "good" English.

1.7. THE LEARNER'S NEEDS AND THE SCOPE OF THE PRESENT STUDY

Every language sorts and classifies speech sounds in different ways. The native speaker's central nervous system has control of the meaningful units and patterns of his language; his muscles have the dexterity to produce its sounds without his conscious attention to them. Native speech habits are so firmly entrenched in the individual that the learning and using of another language are strongly conditioned by them. In the context of cross-cultural communication, allowances are as a rule duly made by the native speaker for the foreigner, whether the latter barely functions with a few halting phrases badly articulated or spouts profusely in an atrocious accent. Many foreigners consider slapdash fluency an acceptable goal, and indeed it is the most that can be expected of many whose firm native speech habits simply cannot be much altered. But some foreigners have the ambition to sound authentic as well as fluent, and under expert guidance they can achieve this goal. It is the clear responsibility of language teachers and textbook writers to provide all learners with the best instruction available, and so to open for all a path toward perfection that they may confidently follow to the limit of their diligence or of their talent.

It is our conviction that the best instruction available in the present day and age is built on a groundwork of scientific analysis. Scientific analysis in this applied field means a thoroughgoing descriptive analysis of both the target and the native language, followed by a point-by-point comparison of the two. A definitive reference work of this sort, giving full coverage in three successive stages to both phonology and grammar, would fill volumes and would require decades to complete. Practical considerations demand that the present volume, designed as it is to strengthen teachers' and textbook writers' hands at this moment, be somewhat streamlined and less than definitively complete. The chapters on phonology, dealing as they do with this relatively finite aspect of language design, first describe that of Italian, then describe that of English, then draw the comparisons, in three separately organized stages. The study of grammar—that almost infinitely complex, open-ended system—is contained in the companion volume THE GRAMMATICAL STRUCTURES OF ENGLISH AND ITALIAN.

THE FIRST LEVEL OF COMPARISON: THE SOUND SYSTEMS

2

2.1. PHONETICS AND THE PHONEME

Phonetics is the study of the exact pronunciation of a language, describing every possible nuance of sound made by the speakers of that language. This "exact" pronunciation is written in a special notation—developed mainly by the International Phonetic Association—and is enclosed in square brackets. Thus one may compile lists of expressions written in their regular spelling and accompanied by phonetic notation, as illustrated for Italian by <u>mezzo</u> ['mɛd-d^{z}o], <u>zio</u> ['t^{s}i:-o], <u>dente</u> ['dɛn^{n}-te], <u>banca</u> ['baŋ^{ŋ}-ka], <u>a cavallo</u> [ak-ka'val-lo].

The value of each phonetic symbol is usually explained in one of two ways: by comparison with a similar sound in another language—for example, [m] as in English <u>ram</u>; or by a close-grained description of the positions and manners of articulation—for example, [m] is articulated by pressing the lips together and letting a stream of air exit through the nasal passages while the vocal cords are in vibration.

The shortcomings of a simple equation of similar sounds in different languages will become obvious in the chapters that follow (Chapter 4 especially). On the other hand, articulatory descriptions of sounds are of great value, and the more accurate they are, the better they serve to point up important differences between languages.

What is lacking, however, in even the closest-grained phonetic descriptions is an exposition of how each speech sound in a language conforms to certain patterns that constitute the PHONOLOGICAL SYSTEM of that language. The system is described by grouping similar sounds together into classes called PHONEMES, and by stating to what extent the DISTRIBUTION (i.e., positions of occurrence) of each sound in a given class is predictable. For example, we establish for Italian a phoneme /n/ (slant lines are used to enclose phonemic notation) which includes, as members of its class, the nasal sounds in both <u>dente</u> and <u>banca</u>. We account for their phonetic differences in terms of their phonetic environments. For example, before members of /k/ phoneme, /n/ is phonetically realize as [ŋ]; before /t/, it is [n]. We can also say that before any stop consonant (/t/, /k/, /g/, etc.), /n/ is realized by a sound which is somewhat longer in duration than elsewhere. (Phonetic length of /n/ is indicated in the notation of our examples dente and banca, given above, by the use of superscript letters.)

Each phoneme symbol therefore subsumes a group of PHONETICALLY SIMILAR sounds and a series of statements defining their ranges of occurrence. Once a speech sound is defined as belonging to a particular phoneme class, it is called an ALLOPHONE, or POSITIONAL VARIANT, of that phoneme.

2.2. MINIMAL PAIRS

A cardinal rule in the identification of a phoneme is that none of its allophones may stand in the same environment and also serve to provide a CONTRAST IN MEANING. For example, the initial sounds of the Italian words rana and lana could not possibly belong to the same phoneme, since they appear in the same environment (initial position and before the same vowel) and are the only sounds which keep these words separate in meaning. On the other hand, it is impossible to find pairs of words in Italian in which only the sounds [n] and [ŋ] serve to convey a difference in meaning. When two words are kept distinct in meaning by one sound alone, they are said to be MINIMAL PAIRS. In the analysis of a language, the discovery of minimal pairs constitutes the most decisive way to determine what the phonemes of a language are. Often, near-minimal pairs present enough proof for phonemic status. For example, it is difficult to find minimal pairs illustrating /ɲ/ (written gn in standard orthography) in contrast with the other phonemes of Italian. This is due to two features of distribution: few words begin with /ɲ/, and /ɲ/ occurs double only in the interior of a word. In one instance, that of /ɲ/ in contrast with /v/, no minimal pairs could be found. Several near-minimal pairs exist, however, such as ragnata /raɲɲáta/ - ravviata /ravviáta/. This evidence, together with the minimal pairs showing /ɲ/ in contrast with all the other phonemes, is sufficient to prove the phonemic status of /ɲ/. (In ¶2.8, we present a list of minimal pairs in Italian.)

2.3. THE PHONEME IN THE CLASSROOM

The teacher reading the above discussion may question the pedagogical value of presenting to the student the sounds of Italian as positional variants of phonemes. The answer involves, in part, the same justification as is given for the teaching of grammatical rules. The student, if he wishes and has time, can go through the long, laborious process of piecemeal assimilation of the foreign language which the infant child follows in learning his native language. If, in order to do this, he places himself in an environment where only the language to be learned is spoken, in a few years he may be speaking the language with a moderate degree of fluency. In the area of pronunciation, his fluency will depend on the extent to which he has learned to produce each speech sound of the foreign language in the environment in which each occurs. If he is in his early teens or younger, his necessarily hit-and-miss approach usually succeeds. If he is older, the growing reluctance to commit errors, which accompanies the maturing of the intellect, hinders him considerably. Also, the older learner is handicapped because the speech habits of his own language are too well formed to be broken easily. Textbooks aid the learner insofar as the presentation of grammatical rules provides an insight into the patterns of the language which otherwise are acquired only through much time and great effort. The distributional statements of sounds as members of phonemes are the phonological equivalents of grammatical rules. They are timesavers to help the student master a foreign pronunciation in a shorter time.

2.4. THE PHONEME IN ENGLISH

So far we have exemplified the phoneme in terms of Italian alone. We have not intended to imply that phoneme classification works only for a few "orderly" languages like Italian. Phonemic analysis is applicable to every language in the world, because the systematic differentiation of utterances through variations in sound is basic to every language. The major phonological differences between languages are those existing between the number and kind of articulations used by each, and the particular inventories of sounds selected by each to convey meaningful contrasts. For example, English has some kinds of articulations that Italian lacks. One such is the puff or air, or ASPIRATION, which accompanies some voiceless stops (example, p, t) in English but not in Italian. To illustrate this special feature of English, try holding a thin sheet of paper close to your mouth while uttering the English word poor a few times. Then say the Italian word porre. You will notice that the paper is blown sharply away from your mouth when you say the English word, but hardly at all when you say the Italian word. If the learner says porre with the characteristic English aspiration of poor, he is marked as having an accent even though the native Italian listener may not be able to explain just what is wrong.

An illustration of the second type of phonological difference between languages can be made by comparing the status of [n] and [ŋ] in Italian and English. In Italian, these are positional variants of the same phoneme /n/. In English, they belong to the separate phonemes /n/ and /ŋ/, since they serve to keep words distinctive in meaning; compare the minimal pairs:

/sín/ sin - /síŋ/ sing
/rə́n/ run - /rə́ŋ/ rung

2.5. WHAT IS A SOUND SYSTEM?

The patterning of speech sounds does not stop with the distribution of positional variants. Having once determined the phonemes of a language, the linguist observes that they pattern with one another in various ways. Although two phonemes by definition differ by at least one articulatory feature, they may share some other feature or features. For example, Italian /b/ and /p/ are significantly different, in that /b/ is VOICED (the vocal cords vibrate during its production), whereas /p/ is VOICELESS (the vocal cords do not vibrate); yet /b/ and /p/ share the feature of BILABIAL CLOSURE. Thus it is possible to state that /b/ and /p/ constitute a PAIR of phonemes, one of which is voiced and the other voiceless. The next step is to discover how many pairs of phonemes can be identified by the voiced-voiceless criterion. In Italian, we find a number beside /b/ and /p/: for example, /d/ and /t/, /g/ and /k/, and others.

Shared features characterize not only pairs of phonemes but SETS of any size. For example, Italian /m/ joins /b/ and /p/ in a bilabial set, whereas /m/, /n/, and /ɲ/ form a NASAL set. Thus /m/ is a member of two sets. Pairs and sets of phonemes are as useful in dealing with a sound system as parts of speech are in stating principles of grammar.

Another way of describing the sound system of a language is in terms of the occurrence of its phonemes in the flow of speech. So viewed, all vowels in Italian constitute a subsystem in that they all occur as the essential ingredient of a syllable. The sequence /fstr/ does not constitute a syllable in Italian, because it does not contain a vowel. This statement is of course made only within the framework of Italian; a syllable has to be separately defined for each language. To avoid an apparent circularity in our definition of the syllable in Italian, we may add that although the syllable must be defined in terms of vowels, vowels do not have to be defined in terms of syllables. As phonemes, they share some features—for example tongue position, which will be discussed in detail in ¶2.6—which clearly define them as a set of vowels.

2.6. THE VOWEL PHONEMES OF ITALIAN

There are three distinctive features of articulation involved in the formation of Italian vowels:

1. TONGUE HEIGHT. By this is meant the relative position of the tongue in its vertical (up-down) motion. In Italian, there are four distinctive heights, called, logically enough, HIGH, HIGHER MID, LOWER MID and LOW.

2. TONGUE HORIZONTAL POSITION. This is perhaps best understood through the analogy of a loose carpet. Besides being able to lift it up and down (cf. tongue height), one can pick it up along any part of its length. In Italian, there are three distinctive areas which can be raised: FRONT, CENTER, and BACK. Therefore, combining horizontal position with tongue height, one could for example have the front part of the tongue in a high position or have the back part of the tongue in a lower mid position, and so on.

3. LIP POSITION. While the front, central, or back part of the tongue is being raised or lowered, the lips are also in motion. In Italian, it is necessary to distinguish two lip positions: either they are ROUNDED (as in saying /u/) or they are UNROUNDED (as in saying /i/).

Of twenty-four possible combinations of the features listed above, Italian selects seven to make up the stock of its vowel phonemes. Each vowel phoneme is listed, with tongue and lip positions also indicated, as follows:

Vowel Phoneme	Tongue Height	Tongue Horizontal Position	Lip Position
/i/	high	front	unrounded
/e/	higher mid	front	unrounded
/ɛ/	lower mid	front	unrounded
/a/	low	center	unrounded
/ɔ/	lower mid	back	rounded
/o/	higher mid	back	rounded
/u/	high	back	rounded

The higher mid vowels are sometimes called "close" and are symbolized ẹ, ọ. The lower mid vowels are sometimes called "open" and are symbolized ę, ǫ.

A feature concomitant with tongue height is ORAL APERTURE. The lower the tongue position, the greater the opening of the mouth. Therefore the mouth is opened widest for /a/ because it has the lowest tongue position, and least widely for /i/ and /u/ because they have the highest tongue positions.

The following statements of distribution account for the occurrences of positional variants.

All stressed vowels are somewhat longer before single consonants than they are before double consonants and other consonant clusters. Thus caro is phonetically ['ka:-ro] with a longer /a/ (indicated by the following two dots), whereas carro is ['kar-ro] with a shorter /a/. Compare also vita ['vi:-ta] with vista ['vis-ta]. Written phonemically, these four examples are simply /káro/, /kárro/, /víta/, and /vísta/.

/i/ and /u/ have the consonant-like variants [y] and [w] respectively before vowels in the same syllable, and the more vowel-like variants [i̯] and [u̯] respectively after vowels in the same syllable—for example, ['yɛ:-ri] ieri, ['wɔ:-vo] uovo; ['mai̯] mai, ['kau̯-za] causa. Phonemically these are /iɛ́ri/, /uɔ́vo/, /mái/, /káusa/.

/e/, /ɛ/, /a/, /ɔ/, and /o/, each has one allophone in all positions, stressed or unstressed.

Vowels are sometimes slightly nasalized before or after a nasal consonant—for example, ['kõ:-me] come, ['lũ:-na] luna, phonemically /kóme/, /lúna/.

A more conventional way of arranging Italian vowels in a diagram is achieved if only tongue height and horizontal position are taken as significant factors:

	front	center	back
high	i		u
higher mid	e		o
lower mid	ɛ		ɔ
low		a	

Still another type of diagram can be drawn to illustrate the ways in which one Italian vowel phoneme is distinct from all the others:

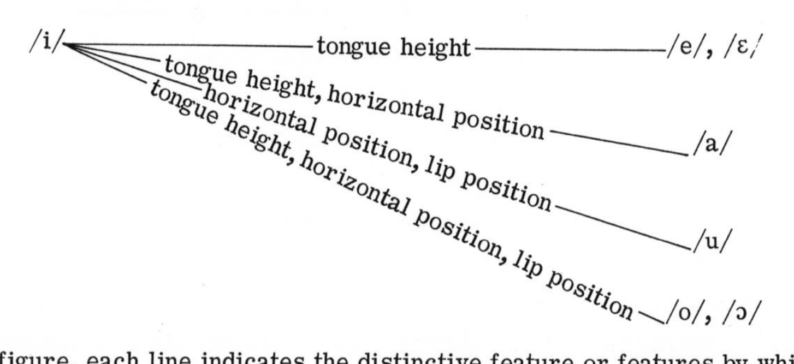

In this figure, each line indicates the distinctive feature or features by which /i/ differs from the other vowels. Keeping the same diagram with the same arrangement of distinctive features, we can substitute all other vowels except /a/ for /i/ in the pivot position:

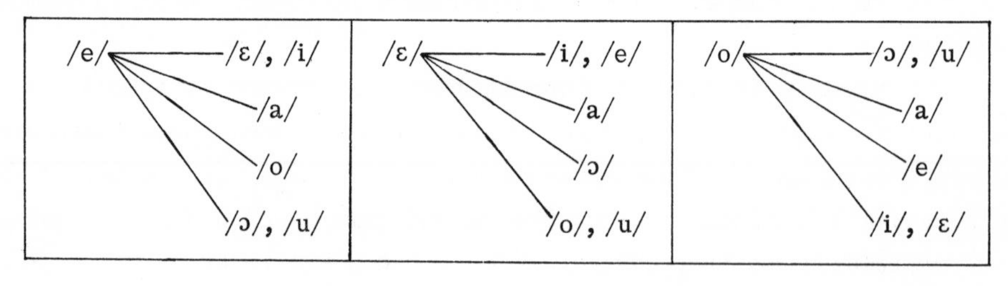

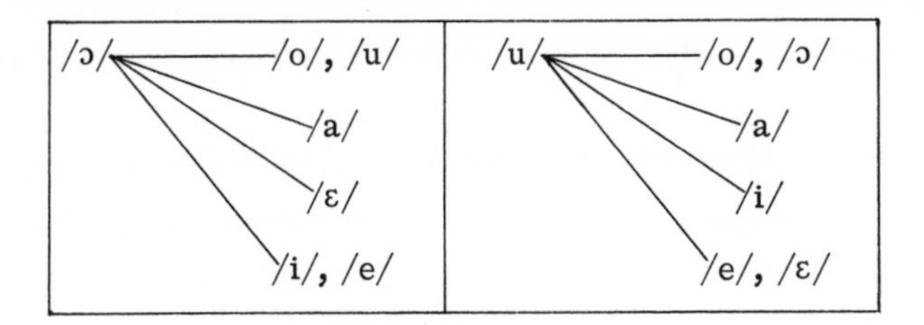

The diagram with /a/ as pivot is different from the others:

/a/ — tongue height, horizontal position — /i/, /e/, /ɛ/
/a/ — tongue height, horizontal position, lip position — /ɔ/, /o/, /u/

This is because /a/ differs from /i/, /e/, and /ɛ/ in two ways (tongue height and horizontal position), and from /ɔ/, /o/, and /u/ in three ways (tongue height, horizontal position, and lip position).

2.7. THE CONSONANT PHONEMES OF ITALIAN

Features of consonant articulation are described somewhat differently from those of vowel articulation. For consonants, we speak of two kinds of distinctive features: MANNER and POSITION. In Italian, there are four contrasts in the manner of articulating consonants:

ORAL or NASAL. If the stream of air is allowed to go through the nasal passage during the articulation of a consonant, the manner is said to be nasal: /m/, /n/, /ɲ/. If the VELIC, or back entrance to the nasal passage, is kept closed, the consonant is said to be oral: /b/, /t/, /ǧ/.

VOICED or VOICELESS. If the vocal cords are made to vibrate during the production of the sound, it is said to be voiced. If not, it is called voiceless. (See ¶ 2.5.)

OCCLUSIVE or CONTINUANT. If the sound involves complete stoppage of the air stream through the mouth during any part of its production, it is defined as an occlusive. Continuant consonants may have more or less constriction of the air passage but, by definition, do not have complete closure.

There are two types of occlusive consonants in Italian: the STOPS /p/, /b/, /t/, /d/, /k/, /g/; and the AFFRICATES /c/, /ʒ/, /č/, /ǧ/. The affricates begin with stop articulation, but instead of being released directly like the stops they are released through an intermediate stage, which may be indicated in phonetic notation by a raised symbol following the stop element. Thus /c/ is phonetically $[t^{s}]$, /ʐ/ is $[d^{z}]$, /č/ is $[t^{\check{s}}]$, and /ǧ/ is $[d^{\check{z}}]$. These affricates are the initial sounds, respectively, of the words zio, zona, cento, gente.

RESTRICTIVE or NON-RESTRICTIVE. If the continuant consonant allows the air to pass through the mouth with comparatively little restriction, it is said to be non-restrictive. Non-restrictive consonants are /l/, /ʎ/, and /r/; /l/ and /ʎ/ are further called laterals, because the air passes over the sides of the tongue; /r/ is known as a trill, because of the tapping of the tongue tip against the ridge behind the upper teeth or ALVEOLAR RIDGE. Restrictive consonants are /f/, /v/, /s/, and /š/, the latter being the initial sound of scende. The term FRICATIVE further describes /f/ and /v/, in which the air stream passes over the flat surface of the lower lip; /s/ and /š/ are SIBILANTS, in the production of which the tongue is somewhat grooved to allow the air to pass through a more or less round opening.

The manners of articulation may be represented schematically:

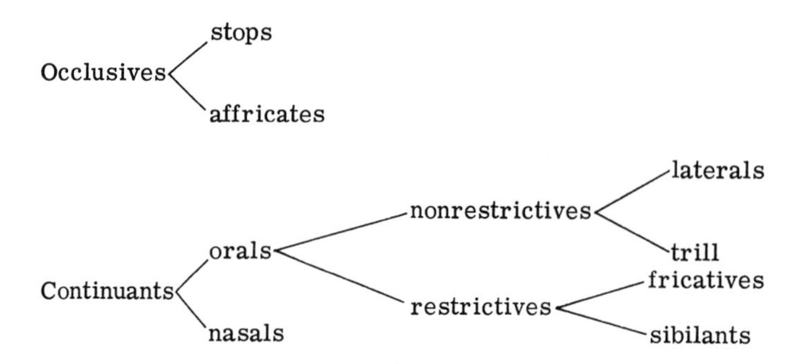

There are five positions of articulation for Italian consonants:

BILABIAL. In the bilabial position, the two lips are pressed together, as in /p/, /b/, /m/.

LABIO-DENTAL. In this position, the lower lip touches the upper front teeth, as in /f/, /v/.

APICO-DENTAL. Here the APEX, or tongue tip, touches the backs of the upper front teeth approximately where they emerge from the gum, as in /t/, /d/, /c/, /ʐ/, /s/, /l/, /r/, /n/.

LAMINO-ALVEOLAR. The LAMINA, or tongue blade (the area just behind the tip) touches the ridge behind the upper teeth as in /č/, /ǧ/, /š/, /ʎ/, /ɲ/.

DORSO-VELAR. The back part of the tongue touches the VELUM or soft palate, which is located just back of the hard palate on the roof of the mouth, as in /k/, /g/

In Italian, there are twenty consonant phonemes resulting from combinations of the manners and positions listed above. The symbols by which they are represented are given below together with their distinctive features and positional variants.

/p/—voiceless bilabial stop: [p], as in pigro, pane

/b/—voiced bilabial stop: [b], as in babbo, bionda

/t/—voiceless apico-dental stop: [t], as in tutto, terra

/d/—voiced apico-dental stop: [d], as in dente, dopo

/k/—voiceless dorso-velar stop: [k̂] (somewhat advanced position of articulation before front vowels), as in chiesa, chimica; elsewhere [k], as in cane, come

/g/—voiced dorso-velar stop: [ĝ] (with the same distribution as [k̂] above), as in ghiaccio, ghigno; elsewhere [g], as in gagliardo, gatto

/c/—voiceless apico-dental affricate: [t^{s}], as in zio, zampa

/z/—voiced apico-dental affricate: [d^{z}], as in zona, zabaione

/č/—voiceless lamino-alveolar affricate: [$t^{\check{s}}$], as in ciao, cicerone

/ǧ/—voiced lamino-alveolar affricate: [$d^{\check{z}}$], as in gentile, gente

/f/—voiceless labio-dental fricative: [f], as in fatto, fiume

/v/—voiced labio-dental fricative: [v], as in vita, vampa

/s/—apico-dental sibilant: [s] , as in sale, sera

All speakers of Italian have a voiced variant [z] before voiced consonants, as in sdraio, sganciare. Most speakers have [s] in all other positions, as in senza, aspetto. A growing number of speakers have [z] within the word between vowels as in casa, sposa. A few speakers have a contrast between [s] and [z] in this position, with [s] in words like risalire and [z] in words like risorgere. For these speakers, [s] and [z] belong to separate phoneme classes. We will consider standard Italian as having [z] before voiced consonants and between vowels and [s] in the other positions.

/š/—lamino-alveolar sibilant: [š], as in scienza, sciupata

/l/—apico-dental lateral: [l], as in lento, luna

/ʎ/—lamino-alveolar lateral: [ʎ], as in gli, figlio

/r/—apico-dental flap: [r], as in regno, ragazzo

/m/—bilabial nasal: [m], as in mamma, marmo, lombardo

/n/—apico-dental nasal: dorso-velar variant [ŋ] before dorso-velar stops, as in banca, bianco; labio-dental variant [ɱ] before /f/ and /v/, as in infamia, invidia; apico-dental [n] elsewhere: nano, nebbia

/ɲ/—lamino-alveolar nasal: [ɲ], as in gnocco, regno

The Italian consonants placed according to their manners and positions of articulation are as follows:

POSITIONS

MANNERS	bilabial	labio-dental	apico-dental	lamino-alveolar	dorso-velar
Stops vls. vd.	p b		t d		k g
Affricates vls. vd.			c ʒ	č ǧ	
Fricatives vls. vd.		f v			
Sibilants			s	š	
Laterals			l	ʎ	
Flap			r		
Nasals	m		n	ɲ	

vls.-voiceless
vd.-voiced

The same type of diagram which was drawn for vowels, above, may also be applied to consonants to illustrate ways in which each consonant phoneme differs from all the others. The following diagram is presented with /p/ as pivot:

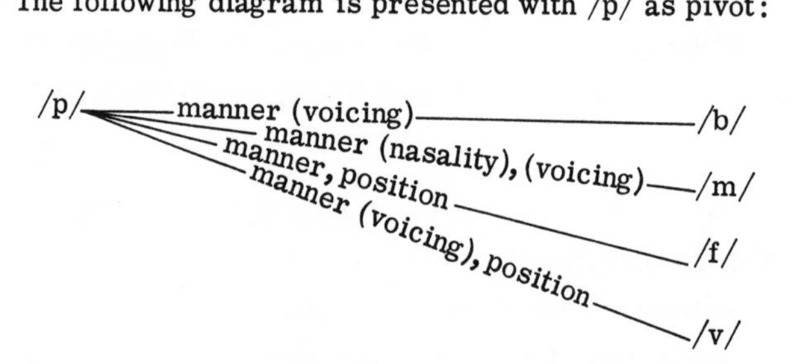

A useful exercise for the student of Italian phonology would be to complete similar diagrams for all the other Italian consonant phonemes.

2.8. ITALIAN MINIMAL PAIRS

The pairs of words listed below serve to justify the establishment of twenty-seven vowel and consonant phonemes in Italian. All pairs are minimal except the two illustrating the contrast between /v/ and /ɲ/ (see ¶ 2.2).

Vowels

/i/ - /e/: ditta - detta
/i/ - /ɛ/: ira - era (noun)
/i/ - /a/: affitto - affatto
/i/ - /ɔ/: fissa - fossa
/i/ - /o/: finte - fonte
/i/ - /u/: fine - fune
/e/ - /ɛ/: venti (twenty) - venti (winds)
/e/ - /a/: ghetta - gatta
/e/ - /ɔ/: legge - logge
/e/ - /o/: mente - monte
/e/ - /u/: melo - mulo
/ɛ/ - /a/: leva - lava
/ɛ/ - /ɔ/: peste - poste
/ɛ/ - /o/: tenda - tonda
/ɛ/ - /u/: gente - giunte
/a/ - /ɔ/: latte - lotte
/a/ - /o/: ara - ora
/a/ - /u/: lana - luna
/ɔ/ - /o/: rocca (fort) - rocca (distaff)
/ɔ/ - /u/: nodo - nudo
/o/ - /u/: rotto - rutto

Consonants

/p/ - /b/: paci - baci
/p/ - /t/: pacco - tacco
/p/ - /d/: petto - detto
/p/ - /k/: pane - cane
/p/ - /g/: pallina - gallina
/p/ - /c/: pio - zio
/p/ - /z̧/: panni - zanni
/p/ - /č/: penare - cenare
/p/ - /ǧ/: pelato - gelato
/p/ - /f/: piccare - ficcare
/p/ - /v/: peste - veste
/p/ - /s/: pacco - sacco
/p/ - /š/: palare - scialare
/p/ - /m/: penare - menare
/p/ - /n/: pascere - nascere
/p/ - /ɲ/: cappa - cagna
/p/ - /l/: panciata - lanciata
/p/ - /ʎ/: mappa - maglia
/p/ - /r/: pane - rane
/b/ - /t/: bordo - tordo
/b/ - /d/: beve - deve
/b/ - /k/: ballo - callo
/b/ - /g/: barbato - garbato
/b/ - /c/: baffo - zaffo
/b/ - /z̧/: belare - zelare
/b/ - /č/: birro - cirro

/b/ - /ǧ/ : busto - giusto
/b/ - /f/ : bollato - follato
/b/ - /v/ : bello - vello
/b/ - /s/ : bella - sella
/b/ - /š/ : bene - scene
/b/ - /m/: banco - manco
/b/ - /n/ : bove - nove
/b/ - /ɲ/ : babbo - bagno
/b/ - /l/ : banda - landa
/b/ - /ʎ/ : babbo - baglio
/b/ - /r/ : banda - randa
/t/ - /d/ : tannato - dannato
/t/ - /k/ : tocco - cocco
/t/ - /g/ : trave - grave
/t/ - /c/ : tappa - zappa
/t/ - /ȥ/ : tonato - zonato
/t/ - /č/ : tingere - cingere
/t/ - /ǧ/ : tenero - genero
/t/ - /f/ : tasto - fasto
/t/ - /v/ : tenuta - venuta
/t/ - /s/ : torte - sorte
/t/ - /š/ : tolto - sciolto
/t/ - /m/: tale - male
/t/ - /n/ : tappo - nappo
/t/ - /ɲ/ : tocco - gnocco
/t/ - /l/ : tira - lira
/t/ - /ʎ/ : ti - gli
/t/ - /r/ : tana - rana
/d/ - /k/ : di - chi
/d/ - /g/ : doccia - goccia
/d/ - /c/ : dannare - zannare
/d/ - /ȥ/ : danni - zanni
/d/ - /č/ : destro - cestro
/d/ - /ǧ/ : dente - gente
/d/ - /f/ : data - fata
/d/ - /v/ : diva - viva

/d/ - /s/ : dente - sente
/d/ - /š/ : dame - sciame
/d/ - /m/: dedica - medica
/d/ - /n/ : deve - neve
/d/ - /ɲ/ : cadde - cagne
/d/ - /l/ : dato - lato
/d/ - /ʎ/ : di - gli
/d/ - /r/ : degno - regno
/k/ - /g/ : crasso - grasso
/k/ - /c/ : coppa - zoppa
/k/ - /ȥ/ : conato - zonato
/k/ - /č/ : chi - ci
/k/ - /ǧ/ : caccio - giaccio
/k/ - /f/ : caro - faro
/k/ - /v/ : canto - vanto
/k/ - /s/ : canto - santo
/k/ - /š/ : cogliere - sciogliere
/k/ - /m/: chi - mi
/k/ - /n/ : come - nome
/k/ - /ɲ/ : cocco - gnocco
/k/ - /l/ : campo - lampo
/k/ - /ʎ/ : chi - gli
/k/ - /r/ : chinato - rinato
/g/ - /c/ : gatta - zatta
/g/ - /ȥ/ : gotico - zotico
/g/ - /č/ : ghigno - cigno
/g/ - /ǧ/ : gallo - giallo
/g/ - /f/ : gatto - fatto
/g/ - /v/ : gola - vola
/g/ - /s/ : gala - sala
/g/ - /š/ : gatto - sciatto
/g/ - /m/: gassoso - massoso
/g/ - /n/ : gasco - nasco
/g/ - /ɲ/ : gaulo - gnaulo
/g/ - /l/ : gotto - lotto
/g/ - /ʎ/ : veggo - veglio

/g/ - /r/ : gazza - razza (spoke)
/c/ - /ʐ/ : razza - razza
/c/ - /č/ : zeppo - ceppo
/c/ - /ǧ/ : pezzo - peggio
/c/ - /f/ : zarina - farina
/c/ - /v/ : zampa - vampa
/c/ - /s/ : zana - sana
/c/ - /š/ : uzzo - uscio
/c/ - /m/: zanna - manna
/c/ - /n/ : zappa - nappa
/c/ - /ɲ/ : puzzo - pugno
/c/ - /l/ : zolla - lolla
/c/ - /ʎ/ : mazza - maglia
/c/ - /r/ : zatta - ratta
/ʐ/ - /č/ : zelare - celare
/ʐ/ - /ǧ/ : zenitale - genitale
/ʐ/ - /f/ : zara - fara
/ʐ/ - /v/ : zinco - vinco
/ʐ/ - /s/ : zonato - sonato
/ʐ/ - /š/ : razza - rascia
/ʐ/ - /m/: zelare - melare
/ʐ/ - /n/ : zona - nona
/ʐ/ - /ɲ/ : razza - ragna
/ʐ/ - /l/ : gazza - galla
/ʐ/ - /ʎ/ : lazzo - l'aglio
/ʐ/ - /r/ : zozza - rozza
/č/ - /ǧ/ : celare - gelare
/č/ - /f/ : cerro - ferro
/č/ - /v/ : cento - vento
/č/ - /s/ : cera - sera
/č/ - /š/ : cenata - scenata
/č/ - /m/: ci - mi
/č/ - /n/ : cervo - nervo
/č/ - /ɲ/ : ciocco - gnocco
/č/ - /l/ : cima - lima
/č/ - /ʎ/ : ci - gli

/č/ - /r/ : cicca - ricca
/ǧ/ - /f/ : giglio - figlio
/ǧ/ - /v/ : gelata - velata
/ǧ/ - /s/ : geminare - seminare
/ǧ/ - /š/ : gialle - scialle
/ǧ/ - /m/: gelato - melato
/ǧ/ - /n/ : gesso - nesso
/ǧ/ - /ɲ/ : leggi - legni
/ǧ/ - /l/ : getto - letto
/ǧ/ - /ʎ/ : maggio - maglio
/ǧ/ - /r/ : getto - retto
/f/ - /v/ : finta - vinta
/f/ - /s/ : folata - solata
/f/ - /š/ : fame - sciame
/f/ - /m/: fai - mai
/f/ - /n/ : fato - nato
/f/ - /ɲ/ : baffi - bagni
/f/ - /l/ : fatte - latte
/f/ - /ʎ/ : baffi - bagli
/f/ - /r/ : fatto - ratto
/v/ - /s/ : vano - sano
/v/ - /š/ : valle - scialle
/v/ - /m/: vano - mano
/v/ - /n/ : vano - nano
/v/ - /ɲ/ : { ravviata - ragnata; scavare - scagnare }
/v/ - /l/ : vento - lento
/v/ - /ʎ/ : vi - gli
/v/ - /r/ : viva - riva
/s/ - /š/ : senza - scienza
/s/ - /m/: santo - manto
/s/ - /n/ : segato - negato
/s/ - /ɲ/ : l'asso - lagno
/s/ - /l/ : seccare - leccare
/s/ - /ʎ/ : massa - maglia

/s/ - /r/ : sotto - rotto
/š/ - /m/: scenata - menata
/š/ - /n/ : sciatta - natta
/š/ - /ɲ/ : sciocco - gnocco
/š/ - /l/ : scialba - l'alba
/š/ - /r/ : cosciente - corrente
/m/- /n/ : modo - nodo
/m/- /ɲ/ : mamma - magna
/m/- /l/ : mesto - lesto
/m/- /ʎ/ : mi - gli
/m/- /r/ : movente - rovente
/n/ - /ɲ/ : l'anno - lagno
/n/ - /ʎ/ : anno - aglio
/n/ - /r/ : natta - ratta
/ɲ/ - /l/ : bagno - ballo
/ɲ/ - /ʎ/ : pugna - puglia
/ɲ/ - /r/ : bagna - barra
/l/ - /ʎ/ : lî - gli
/l/ - /r/ : lido - rido
/ʎ/ - /r/ : sbaglia - sbarra

2.9. THE PHONEMES OF ENGLISH

The treatment of the phonemes of English will be somewhat more succinct tha that given the Italian phonemes above. To a certain extent this is possible because the re erence frames established above remain relatively unchanged.

2.9.1. ENGLISH VOWEL NUCLEI

Here we make one chief departure from the method used to describe Italian vowels. Because of the phonetic characteristics of English vowels, we find it advantageou to speak of vowel nuclei rather than merely of vowels. The term VOWEL NUCLEUS is intended to cover arrangements of vowels and vowel-like sounds in the English spoken by most Americans. To illustrate, let us compare the Italian vowel /i/ in filo with the vowel nucleus of the English word feel. The two differ in a crucial way. In Chapter 3 we discuss this difference in detail, but let it suffice for now to say that the vowel nucleus represented by ee in the word feel consists of not one but two phonemic entities: a vowel which we represent with the symbol /i/ as in Italian, and a VOCALIC OFF GLIDE or SEMIVOWEL which we represent with the symbol /y/. Whereas our phonemic notation of the Italian example would be /fílo/, the English word would be written /fíyl/. In English, there are altogether fourteen vowel nuclei. Seven of these are like /iy/ in feel in that the end with an off glide. Seven are like the vowel nucleus of fill, which does not contain an off glide; phonemically, fill is written /fíl/. Phonetically, /fíl/ differs from /fíyl/ in mor than just the absence of an off glide. The other phonetic differences are discussed below under distinctive features of the vowel nuclei (¶2.9.1.1). Also, more important for this study is a further problem which for the present can be raised only in the form of a question: Which of the two vowel nuclei /i/ or /iy/ is more similar to Italian vowel /i/? A related question is: How is the learning of Italian vowels by our students affected by the vowel nuclei of their native English? The answers are best delayed until after the discussion of English phonemes (Chapters 3, 4).

The fourteen vowel nuclei of English are:

/iy/ as in beat	/ay/ as in bite
/i/ as in bit	/ə/ as in but
/ey/ as in bait	/o/ as in bought
/e/ as in bet	/ow/ as in boat
/ae/ as in bat	/u/ as in put
/a/ as in bot	/uw/ as in boot
/aw/ as in bout	/oy/ as in boy

We do not offer a separate list of minimal pairs to verify the establishment of the English vowel nuclei, since all the above examples except put and boy function in that capacity. It is not difficult to find additional pairs showing a contrast of the nuclei of put and boy with all the others; for example, put - pit, put - pet, put - pat, or boy - bee, boy - bah, boy - bey, and so on.

2.9.1.1. DISTINCTIVE FEATURES OF THE VOWEL NUCLEI

The English vowel system contains the same distinctive features of articulation found in the Italian system. Just as in Italian, there are four tongue heights, three horizontal positions of the tongue, and two positions of the lips. The PHONEMIC differences are to be found in the different arrangements of these features. The PHONETIC differences are defined in Chapter 3 in terms of relative tongue height, horizontal position, and lip position.

The seven simple vowel nuclei (those not containing an off glide), arranged on the model of the description of Italian vowels in ¶ 2.6, follow:

Vowel Nuclei	Tongue Height	Tongue Horizontal Position	Lip Position
/i/	high	front	unrounded
/e/	higher mid	front	unrounded
/ae/	lower mid	front	unrounded
/a/	low	central	unrounded
/o/	lower mid	back	rounded
/u/	high	back	rounded
/ə/	mid	central	unrounded

The off glides /y/ and /w/ have the same features as /i/ and /u/ respectively. Their phonetic differences are in terms of RELATIVE PROMINENCE—that is, /y/ and /w/ are never as prominent either in length or in volume as /i/ and /u/. Their phonemic differences must be explained in terms of their PRIVILEGES OF OCCURRENCE—that is they are assigned phonemic status because the differences between sequences like /yi/ (as in /yip/ yip) and /iy/ (as in /iyt/ eat), and /wu/ (as in /wud/ wood) and /uw/ (as in /buw/ boo) could not be indicated if [y] and [w] were considered only as positional variants of /i/ and /u/. There are several alternative solutions to the phonemic writing of these sequences, but this one was chosen because it facilitates comparison with Italian.

The phoneme /ə/ is listed as having a tongue height describable only as mid, because actually it ranges from lower to higher mid.

All fourteen vowel nuclei are tabulated below. As before, lip position is not indicated. (In both languages, all front vowels are unrounded and all back vowels are rounded.) The higher mid location of /ow/ and /oy/ is due to the presence of the off glides /w/ and /y/. There are, however, many speakers for whom /ow/, /oy/ and /o/ are all lower mid.

	front	center	back
high	iy i		uw u
higher mid	ey e	ə	ow, oy
lower mid	ae		o
low		a aw, ay	

Positional variants of English vowel nuclei vary to a certain extent from region to region. The following statement is to be read with this understanding. Generally speaking, in the articulation of /i/, /e/, /o/, /u/, the tongue is somewhat lower in the mouth than in /iy/, /ey/, /ow/, /oy/, and /uw/, respectively.

All vowel nuclei tend to be somewhat shorter before voiceless consonants than before voiced consonants. Compare bit - bid, bite - bide, pate - paid, and so on. Some varieties of American English introduce length as a phonemic entity in such pairs as can (be able) - can (preserve food). Other dialect areas (eastern New England, for example) use length as a positional variant of the consonant /r/ as in the pair pot - part (['pat] - ['pa:t] instead of ['pat] - ['part]).

2.9.2. ENGLISH CONSONANT PHONEMES

The consonants of English may be described almost wholly within the framework we have used for Italian consonants. There is one new position of articulation to be added to the stock of Italian positions: *apico-alveolar*. This is the position in which the tip of the tongue touches or approaches the ridge behind the upper teeth. English /t/ and /d/ have this position in the speech of most Americans, whereas Italian /t/ and /d/ are generally apico-dental. The phonemes /h/ and /r/ are discussed separately below. The phonemes /w/ and /y/ are termed consonants in their occurrence before vowel nuclei, because in this position they pattern like all the other consonant phonemes, and in forceful articulation have the phonetic features of fricative consonants (try saying the words *you* and *witch* with great emphasis and speed).

The consonants of English with their distinctive features are the following:

/p/—voiceless bilabial stop, as in *pin*, *pop*
/b/—voiced bilabial stop, as in *bin*, *bob*
/t/—voiceless apico-alveolar stop, as in *tin*, *tot*
/d/—voiced apico-alveolar stop, as in *did*, *dot*
/k/—voiceless dorso-velar stop, as in *kin*, *kick*
/g/—voiced dorso-velar stop, as in *gain*, *gun*
/č/—voiceless lamino-alveolar affricate, as in *chin*, *church*
/ǧ/—voiced lamino-alveolar affricate, as in *gin*, *job*
/f/—voiceless labio-dental fricative, as in *fin*, *fop*
/v/—voiced labio-dental fricative, as in *vim*, *vat*
/θ/—voiceless apico-dental fricative, as in *thin*, *thigh*
/ð/—voiced apico-dental fricative, as in *then*, *that*
/s/—voiceless apico-alveolar sibilant, as in *see*, *saw*
/z/—voiced apico-alveolar sibilant, as in *zero*, *rose*
/š/—voiceless lamino-alveolar sibilant, as in *shy*, *shoe*
/ž/—voiced lamino-alveolar sibilant, as in *vision*, *pleasure*
/l/—apico-alveolar lateral, as in *leek*, *look* } (see below for
/r/—apico-alveolar continuant, as in *rim*, *run* } more discussion)
/m/—bilabial nasal, as in *meek*, *mother*
/n/—apico-alveolar nasal, as in *none*, *name*
/ŋ/—dorso-velar nasal, as in *sing*, *long*
/h/—aspiration, as in *hit*, *hat*, *hut* (see below for more discussion)

Two phonemes in English require special consideration: /h/ and /r/.

The significant feature of /h/ is aspiration or the release of a breathy-sounding stream of air. Its positional variants are conditioned, or "colored," by the surrounding sounds. To illustrate, compare the initial sounds of the words hot and hit. If you whisper them, you will notice that the positions of articulation do not change as you pass from the initial sound to the vowel sound. The only difference is a noticeable decrease in the degree of breathiness. Consequently, one might be tempted to call English /h/ a voic less vowel. It certainly does not have the marked oral friction of /h/–like phonemes in other languages (cf. the Spanish jota sound). We choose to call it a consonant, however, again on the grounds that it patterns like the other consonants (consonant and vowel patterning will be discussed in detail in Chapters 4 and 5); furthermore, to do so facilitates our comparisons with Italian.

The continuant /r/ is somewhat more difficult to classify. Its articulation involves little restriction or friction in the mouth. There is no contact between the tongue and any part of the roof of the mouth. In pre-vocalic /r/, the tongue is retroflexed (bent backward), with the tip just behind the alveolar ridge. There is also noticeable lip rounding when it occurs at the beginnings of words, as will be clearly evident if you stand befo a mirror and say the words run, ram, right, rim, red. It is possibly this lip rounding which causes many English-speaking children to confuse /r/ with /w/ and to say "wun" for run, "wabbit" for rabbit, and so on.

The bulk of the articulatory evidence points to assigning /r/ to the vowels. The only phonetic support for calling it a consonant comes from those dialects of Americ and British English that pronounce /r/ with a flap of the tongue against either the backs o the upper teeth or the alveolar ridge, as in the word three or (in the British Isles) in the words merry, very, and so on.

But again we have other good reasons for calling /r/, like /h/, a consonant: patterning, and facilitation of subsequent comparisons with Italian.

The consonants of English are tabulated below according to their manner and position of articulation:

	Bilabial	Labio-dental	Apico-dental	Apico-alveolar	Lamino-alveolar	Dorso-velar
Stops vls. vd.	p b			t d		k g
Affricates vls. vd.					č ǧ	

	Bilabial	Labio-dental	Apico-dental	Apico-alveolar	Lamino-alveolar	Dorso-velar
Fricatives vls. vd.		f v	θ ð			
Sibilants vls. vd.				s z	š ž	
Laterals				l		
Nasals	m			n		ŋ

(For reasons already made apparent, /w/, /y/, /h/, and /r/ do not fit this table and are consequently omitted.) The following statements of distribution hold for the positional variants of the English consonants.

Stops (/p/, /b/, /t/, /d/, /k/, /g/) are not usually released when they occur in word-final position—that is to say, the position of articulation is formed but not distinctly released. Compare the initial sound of pill with the final sound of lip, for example. Whereas the /p/ of pill is always clearly released, the /p/ of lip may not be. Compare similarly ball with lab, dill with lid, car with rack, goal with log.

In everyday American speech, the stops /t/ and /d/ do not always have separate positional variants between a stressed vowel and an unstressed vowel. In this environment the position of articulation of both phonemes is taken and released with such rapidity that the distinctive feature of voicing is often obliterated. To illustrate, say the two words latter and ladder a few times to a listener and then ask him to repeat the sequence in which you have said them. If you speak them in the normal way, the chances are that he will have difficulty recognizing a distinction. Only in deliberate, consciously careful speech are they kept apart.

The voiceless stops /p/, /t/, /k/ and the voiceless affricate /č/ are pronounced with a puff of air (ASPIRATION) when they occur as the first sounds in stressed syllables, except when they follow /s/. Hold a thin sheet of paper close to your mouth while saying the words pin, tick, kin; then compare the action of the paper when you say spin, stick, skin.

All voiced consonants in English start with a slight phase of voicelessness—that is, vibration of the vocal cords begins somewhat later than the other articulatory movements. Listen to yourself carefully while you compare the English word bob with the Italian word babbo; you will notice that the initial sound in the Italian word is fully voiced from the beginning whereas the English word is not. If you are still unconvinced, lightly place two fingers on your throat in the vicinity of the vocal cords and try the two words again. You should be able to feel the vocal cords start to vibrate sooner in the Italian word *babbo*.

The lateral /l/ has two outstanding positional variants in English. They are called, impressionistically, "bright" [l] and "dark" [ɫ]. The articulatory difference is to be found primarily in the position of the tongue. The back of the tongue is somewhat higher in articulation of dark [ɫ]. Its occurrence is limited to syllable-final position, as in the words *table, full, Bill, Tilden*.

Bright [l] occurs elsewhere. Compare the initial sounds of the following words with those above: *like, look, leak, lack, luck*. As we will see below in our comparisons with Italian, the English-speaking student often has difficulty in avoiding a "dark" [ɫ] in Italian words like *il, del, caldo, altro*.

2.10. STRESS AND OTHER "SIMULTANEOUS" PHONEMES

In addition to phonemes of the vowel and consonant type described above, languages have phonemes which occur simultaneously with other phonemes. For example, a relatively greater VOLUME or LOUDNESS of one vowel or vowel nucleus in a word marks it as distinctive from the others. If this increase in loudness is connected with a difference in meaning, we must recognize it as having phonemic status. An English example of this can be found in comparing the words *permit* (noun) and *permit* (verb). In Italian, we find pairs like *canto* and *cantò*. This greater degree of loudness is called STRESS, and we say that both English and Italian have PHONEMIC STRESS. More about stress and a comparison of English and Italian stress is to be found in Chapter 4 (*Comparing Vowel Patterns*).

Another type of simultaneous phoneme is PITCH. Besides increasing or decreasing the loudness of a vowel, one may also pronounce it at different pitches. The arrangement of pitches in an utterance is called an INTONATION PATTERN. The type of meaning conveyed by variations in pitch depends on the individual language. In Chinese, for example, every word is spoken with a characteristic pitch which, if varied, may change the meaning of the word. In both English and Italian, on the other hand, pitch variations are not so closely connected with the word. In these languages the same sequence of words may be said with several different intonation patterns. The English sentence *You're putting that on your head* may be said as a statement of fact, a question, an expression of disbelief, of disgust, or even of horror. With somewhat different arrangements of pitch, the same sorts of meaning are conveyed in Italian. In fact, the importance of mastering proper Italian intonation cannot be emphasized enough. It has been demonstrated that no matter how thoroughly a student commands the other aspects of pronunciation and the grammar of a language, he will always have an "accent" in the ears of native speakers as long as he does not use their intonations. On the other hand, a control of intonation by the student may easily obscure his inabilities in the other areas. People often listen more closely to the way you say things than to what you are saying. Comedians like Danny Kaye and Sid Caesar have contrived entire comedy routines in which they give the impression of speaking a foreign language chiefly by uttering nonsense with the intonation patterns characteristic of that language.

Unfortunately, the teaching of proper intonation is neglected in most classes of elementary Italian. With this in mind, we devote an entire chapter to a comparison and discussion of intonation in Italian and English (Chapter 6).

A third type of phoneme is JUNCTURE. Because of its special features, a part of Chapter 4 (¶4.8) is devoted to defining juncture and comparing English and Italian types.

COMPARING PHONEMES AND THEIR POSITIONAL VARIANTS

3

3.0. THE FIRST STAGE OF COMPARISON

We consider the comparison of the English and Italian sound systems to require two stages. The first is a contrasting of those areas in which the phonemes of the two languages differ. This involves differences between the two languages in both articulation and arrangement of positional variants. The second stage consists of the comparison of phoneme patterns, involving especially differences in syllable and word structure. The present chapter is devoted to the first stage, and is limited to a discussion of vowel and consonant phonemes. Differences in stress phonemes and their arrangements have been reserved for Chapter 4, along with a discussion of English juncture and its interference in learning Italian. Intonation patterns and pitch phonemes occupy the entirety of Chapter 6.

3.1. COMPARING VOWELS

The student's tendency is to interpret Italian vowel phonemes in terms of the positional variants of his English vowel nuclei. We begin by pairing off each Italian vowel phoneme with the English vowel nucleus (or nuclei) which bears the greatest phonetic similarity to it:

	Italian	English
(1)	/i/	/iy/, /i/
(2)	/e/	/ey/
(3)	/ɛ/	/e/, /ae/
(4)	/a/	/a/, /ə/, /ae/
(5)	/ɔ/	/o/
(6)	/o/	/ow/
(7)	/u/	/uw/, /u/

The English vowel nuclei /aw/, /ay/, and /oy/ are omitted from the list because they are similar phonetically to the Italian sequences /au/, /ai/, and /oi/ which are discussed together with other vowel sequences in Chapter 4. Substitution of /ə/ for other vowels in unstressed positions is also discussed in Chapter 4. Observe that English /ae/ is entered in both row 3 and 4 above; its similarities to both /ɛ/ and /a/ are pointed out below.

Having established the correspondences listed above, our next step is to determine the extent of similarity between the Italian vowel and its English counterparts.

1. Italian /i/ - English /iy/, /i/. Italian /i/ has approximately the same tongue height and lip position as English /iy/. The outstanding difference is the lack of an off glide in the Italian vowel. English /i/, although it also lacks an off glide, is considerably lower in tongue position than Italian /i/.

From these observations one might conclude that the English-speaking student has a free choice for mispronouncing Italian /i/; theoretically, he might substitute either his /iy/ or his /i/ for Italian /i/, with no restrictions. There is, however, another phonetic characteristic to be considered in both languages. The Italian vowel /i/ (along with all the others) is phonetically short before two or more consonants, and long before one consonant. English /i/ is phonetically shorter than /iy/, even before voiced consonants (compare bid and bead). Consequently, the student is likely to use his /i/ in Italian words like mille or affitto, where he hears a shorter vowel, and his /iy/ in words like mila, vino, fine, where the vowel is phonetically longer.

2. Italian /e/ - English /ey/. Comparing Italian /e/ and English /ey/, we find that the points of phonetic similarity and difference are identical to those between Italian /i/ and English /iy/. The major distinction to be made in this instance is that English /ey/ is the only vowel nucleus which bears phonetic similarity to Italian /e/. English /e/ is phonetically closer to Italian /ɛ/ than to Italian /e/. Consequently, the student is not likely to substitute English /e/ for Italian /e/ because of phonetic similarity.

3. Italian /ɛ/ - English /e/, /ae/. Although /e/ is tabulated, above, as a higher mid vowel, contrasting with /ae/ which is lower mid, comparison with Italian /ɛ/ shows that English /e/ is phonetically closer to the Italian vowel than is English /ae/. Compare English Ben with Italian bene. You will notice that the tongue is slightly higher in bene. The lips are almost in the same position for both vowels, and the horizontal position of the tongue seems about equal. But now compare bene with English ban; you will notice that the tongue is distinctly lower in ban. English-speaking students will usually substitute English /e/ for Italian /ɛ/. Actually, this is to be encouraged, provided they also reproduce phonetic length before single consonants. There is, however, a tendency

among some students to substitute English /ae/ for Italian /ɛ/. This results mainly from an effort to emphasize the difference in tongue height between Italian /e/ and /ɛ/.

4. Italian /a/ - English /a/, /ə/, /ae/. Of the three English vowel nuclei cited, the first is the most similar to Italian /a/. In the articulation of both Italian and English /a/, the tongue lies fairly low and central in the mouth. In neither instance is there lip rounding. In unstressed positions—especially word-final—English-speaking students have a tendency to substitute /ə/ for Italian /a/, as in Roma, cara, donna. Two factors are at work here. The first is that /ə/ is separated from /a/ by only one distinctive feature: tongue height. This means that /ə/'s closest phonemic neighbor is /a/. The second factor is one of vowel patterning: /ə/ often substitutes for other unstressed vowels in English. Thus the student's use of /ə/ for /a/ in Italian is the result of his substituting a phonetically similar sound in a familiar pattern. More on the transference of patterns and its contribution to pronunciation errors is contained in Chapters 4 and 5.

/ae/ shares less phonetic resemblance with Italian /a/ than does either of the other two English vowel nuclei in question; the number of errors in substituting /ae/ for Italian /a/ is therefore proportionally lower. It may well be that the few errors that do occur are caused primarily by writing interference: /ae/ is spelled almost invariably with the letter a in English. (Compare this with at least four variations of spelling /a/ in English: a as in father, o as in mop (for most Americans), ea as in heart, and e as in sergeant.) As mentioned above, /ae/ replaces /ɛ/ for clearly phonetic reasons.

5. Italian /ɔ/ - English /o/. The somewhat higher tongue position of the Italian vowel seems to be the chief articulatory difference between the two, in addition to the Italian pattern of phonetic length versus shortness which the student must learn to control in the production of all vowels.

6. Italian /o/ - English /ow/. As in the comparison of Italian /e/ and English /ey/, the main difference (and student problem) is the absence of an off glide in Italian /o/ and its presence in English /ow/. It is indeed one of the major tasks of the teacher to train his students to pronounce vowels long without an accompanying off glide. Italian /o/ is also somewhat more rounded than English /ow/.

7. Italian /u/ - English /uw/, /u/. In addition to the off glide and phonetic length problem, the student may have difficulty remembering to round his lips sufficiently for Italian /u/. English /uw/ has the approximate tongue height of Italian /u/ but without the off glide. English /u/ has no off glide, but is distinctly lower and somewhat more centered. Neither /uw/ nor /u/ is as rounded as Italian /u/ (compare English loop, loon with Italian lupo, luna). Fortunately, lip rounding is easily observed and therefore comparatively easy to acquire.

The relative positions (except for lip-rounding) of Italian and English vowels are schematically represented below, according to the articulatory data presented above:

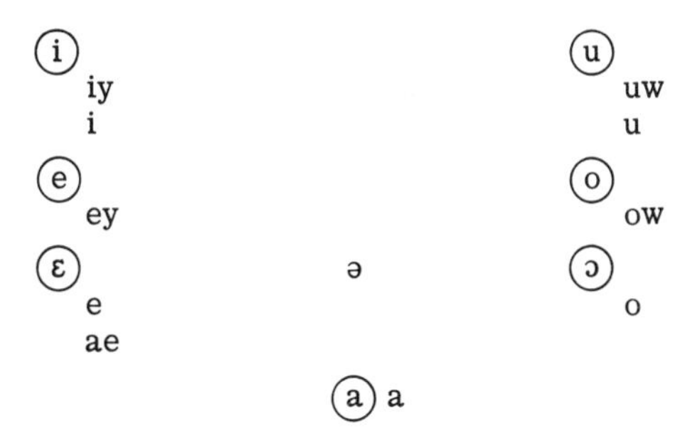

(Italian vowels are circled)

The location of the Italian vowels (circled) to the left of the English vowel nuclei is not intended to be illustrative of any distinctions. On the other hand, vertical spacing is meant to indicate relative similarities and differences. Italian /i/, for example, is higher than English /iy/; English /ae/ is more similar to Italian /ɛ/ than to Italian /a/, and so on.

3.2. COMPARING CONSONANTS

Applying the similarity test to Italian and English consonants, we obtain the following results.

For Italian /p, b, t, d, k, g, č, ǧ, f, v, m, n, s, š, l, r/, there are corresponding English phonemes. Differences in positional variants across language boundaries are covered in the following statements.

Aspiration of initial stops and /č/ in English is not paralleled by Italian. In view of the high frequency of occurrence of stops in both languages, this should be pointed out early in the course of study. The test with paper in front of the mouth, mentioned earlier to illustrate aspiration in English and the lack of it in Italian, is a useful technique in the classroom.

The voicing of /b, d, g/ begins somewhat later in the English phonemes than in the corresponding Italian set. Although this is not a critical distinction, it should be pointed out early in any course in which standards of pronunciation are high. A helpful procedure is to have the student try to set his vocal cords to vibrating (as if humming) a split second before he pronounces the voiced stop. Since his voicing is somewhat delayed by the nature of his English habits, the attempted pre-voicing will more nearly coincide with the beginning of the other articulatory movements.

The position of articulation of English /t/ and /d/ is apico-alveolar, and ther fore farther back in the mouth than the apico-dental position of Italian /t/ and /d/. This is relatively unimportant in the acquiring of native-like pronunciation, because the audib differences are slight. Moreover, there are some speakers of Italian (notably Romans) who pronounce /t/ and /d/ in the apico-alveolar position.

Much more important is keeping Italian /t/ and /d/ distinct intervocalically (between vowels). The merging of latter and ladder, mentioned in Chapter 2, must not be carried over into Italian. Students must be trained early to keep distinct the internal consonants of words like vita, fede, lato, modo.

The "dark" variant of English /l/ has no equivalent in Italian. The tendency is to substitute it for Italian syllable-final /l/ in il, alto, and so on.

Italian /r/ is a trill consonant, whereas English /r/ has partly vowel-like variants (see the discussion on English consonants in Chapter 2). Consequently, Italian /r/ is a difficult sound for Americans to imitate. The teacher might start drill on /r/ by comparing it with the /r/ in English three (although this would not work for everybody or even with the intervocalic /t/ and /d/ in words like latter and ladder which, when articulated rapidly, are similar to Italian /r/. Compare the word today with Italian tre.

The following pairs are either unmatched or imperfectly matched:

	Italian	English
1.	/c/	/ts/
2.	/ʐ/	/dz/
3.	/ɲ/	—
4.	/ʎ/	—
5.	[ŋ] of /n/	/ŋ/
6.	[z] of /s/	/z/
7.	—	/ž/
8.	—	/θ/
9.	—	/ð/
10.	—	/h/

Equivalents for Italian /ɲ/ and /ʎ/ could be added in the English column if we admitted an over-rapid pronunciation of the English sequences /ny/ and /ly/ in words lik onion and million. In rapid speech, /ny/ and /ly/ often have phonetic effects similar to those of /ɲ/ and /ʎ/.

1. Italian /c/, /ʐ/ and English /ts/, /dz/. As far as articulation is concerne the English sequences /ts/ and /dz/ are sufficiently similar phonetically to Italian /c/

and /ʒ/ to allow their use as models for learning the pronunciation of their Italian counterparts. The important differences are to be found essentially in their distribution in both languages—that is, the English sequences /ts/ and /dz/ occur either in word-final positions (as in pats, pads) or, less fequently, across syllable boundaries (as in Patsy, sudsy). Italian /c/ and /ʒ/, on the other hand, occur at the beginnings of words (zio, zona), but only doubled across syllable boundaries (pazzo, mezzo) and never in word-final position. Consequently, there is little overlap in the distributions of Italian /c, ʒ/ versus English /ts, dz/, and it is difficult to train students to pronounce words like zio and zona with these initial phonemes. The tendency will be to substitute the next most similar sound in English, which is /s/ in the case of /c/, and /z/ in the instance of /ʒ/ in word-initial position. If written materials are being used for pronunciation practice, the substitution of English /z/ for Italian /c/ also occurs. This is due mainly to orthographic interference from English (cf. words like zip, zinc, Zion).

2. Italian /ɲ/, /ʎ/—lacking in English. As mentioned above, English /ny/ and /ly/ can be pronounced rapidly so as to approach Italian /ɲ/ and /ʎ/. The learner's articulation of /ʎ/ may be improved further by instruction to press more of the front part of the tongue (LAMINAL SURFACE) against the ridge behind the upper teeth (ALVEOLAR RIDGE) and to hold it there while allowing the air stream to pass over the sides of the tongue. It seems that the articulation of English /l/ (including "bright" [l]) involves somewhat less tongue-ridge contact than English /n/.

Even after acquiring a degree of control over the articulation of /ʎ/, some learners will persist in saying something like [ʎi], thereby making figlio, paglia, and the like three-syllable words. This tendency may be partly reinforced by an interference from the spelling system of Italian, which represents /ʎ/ by writing gli.

3. Italian [ŋ] and English /ŋ/. This is one of two instances (the other being [z]) where a phonetic distinction in Italian is matched by a phonemic one in English. The occurrence of [ŋ] in Italian is completely predictable in terms of surrounding sounds: Italian [ŋ] occurs as the only nasal sound before /k/ or /g/, but nowhere else. English /ŋ/ has a variant which occurs before /k/ or /g/ in the same type of distribution (as in think, linger), but it also has a variant which contrasts with /n/—for example, sin - sing. Since the whole range of occurrence of the positional variant in Italian is found also in English, there is no problem for the learner. The phonemic contrast /n/ - /ŋ/ of English interferes in no way with the control of the [ŋ] allophone in Italian.

4. Italian [z] and English /z/. As in the instance of [ŋ] and /ŋ/, the articulation of Italian [z] is almost identical to that of English /z/. But unlike the previous instance, the distribution of Italian [z] differs from that of English /z/ in one highly impor-

tant way. This difference concerns the phonetics of Italian clusters like /sb, sg, sd, sdr, and will be discussed in Chapter 5.

5. English /ž/, /θ/, /ð/, and /h/ have no parallels either in the phonemic stock of Italian or in any of its positional variants. As a result they cause no problems of pronunciation in the learning of Italian.

3.3. THE PHONEME AND THE WRITING SYSTEM

One of the main problems English-speaking persons have in studying their own language is spelling. This is because the central drive to write the sounds of English sensibly has been sidetracked many times by various and sundry counterdrives. These counterdrives include the efforts of philological purists who have insisted on inserting a b in a word like debt (because Latin debita is its ultimate source), and of medieval Dutch printers alleged to have first spelled ghost with an h. Periods of rapid change in the language have left spelling lagging behind. These include periods of no uniformity at all and yet a constant reluctance ever to change the basic alphabet originally adapted from the Latin. The net result is that English spelling is saddled with an inordinate number of irregularities.

The situation in Italian spelling is completely different. Although Italian spelling does not represent Italian phonemes in a perfect one-to-one relationship, it nevertheless is close enough to provide a striking contrast with English. The list of Italian phonemes and their spellings is given below not only to illustrate this point but also to provide a ready reference for those readers who are not yet completely familiar with phonemic notation.

Phonemes	Traditional Spellings
/i/	i
/e/	e
/ɛ/	e
/a/	a
/ɔ/	o
/o/	o
/u/	u
/p/	p
/b/	b
/t/	t
/d/	d
/k/	c, ch, q

Phonemes	Traditional Spellings
/g/	g, gh
/f/	f
/v/	v
/c/	z
/ʒ/	z
/č/	c (before i, e), ci (before o, a, u)
/ǧ/	g (before i, e), gi (before o, a, u)
/s/	s
/š/	sc (before i, e), sci (before o, a, u)
/l/	l
/ʎ/	gli
/r/	r
/m/	m
/n/	n
/ɲ/	gn

COMPARING VOWEL PATTERNS 4

4.0. THE SECOND STAGE OF COMPARISON

We have discussed the differences encountered by English-speaking students in mastering the phoneme classes of Italian and in pronouncing their positional variants. This we considered to be the first stage of comparison. With the present chapter we beg the second stage: a comparison of the patterns, or distributional arrangements, of the phonemes of Italian and English.

Acquiring near-native pronunciation of a foreign language does not consist entirely of controlling the articulation of new phonemes. This is because languages diffe not only in the number and kind of sounds they use but also in the ways they use them. Consequently, the student who has an excellent control of individual Italian sounds may st have difficulty in pronouncing them in sequence (e.g., in words like *cuoio*, *sgelare*). He may also find it difficult to reproduce the correct stress patterns in words like *índicano* or *opportunità*. Whereas differences in sounds are often anticipated by the beginner, he i seldom prepared for differences in patterns. Yet such differences are not to be underrat

We begin our treatment of patterns with the vowels. We use as our first refe ence frame the smallest unit of patterning in both languages: the syllable. Next we take up what we called SIMULTANEOUS PHONEMES in Chapter 2, and introduce the second u of patterning: the word.

4.1. THE SYLLABLE

We have already partly defined the syllable as the smallest unit of patterning We might rephrase this statement and say that the syllable is the shortest segment of speech pronounceable in a language. Although the stock of sounds in a language may con- tain many types of vowels and consonants, not all of them may occur as syllables. In bot English and Italian, only vowel sounds may occur as the sole members of separate pronounceable syllables. Consonants in both languages may occur in syllables only if they are accompanied by a vowel sound. Even when a consonant letter of the alphabet is named, it is accompanied by a vowel and thereby made a pronounceable unit.

Phonetically speaking, each syllable contains a PEAK OF PROMINENCE. In both English and Italian, this peak may consist of a vowel sound alone or a sequence of vowel sounds. In English, we have the sequence /oy/, for example, which consists of a vowel /o/ and a semi-vowel /y/. Italian /oi/ consists of two vowel phonemes. In both examples, the first sound is more prominent than the second.

The occurrence of consonants in both English and Italian is limited to what are called the SYLLABLE MARGINS. There are two syllable margins. The one preceding the vocalic peak of prominence is called the ONSET, and the one following the peak is called the CODA. A sequence of two or more consonants in either margin is called a CLUSTER. Whereas each syllable must contain a peak, one or both margins may be missing. If we use the symbol C to represent consonants and consonant clusters, and the symbol V to represent vowels and semi-vowels, we may illustrate the four possible types of syllable in the following way:

V (peak alone)
CV (onset plus peak)
CVC (onset plus peak plus coda)
VC (peak plus coda)

Since both English and Italian have all four syllable types, the points of difference are limited to the following:

permissible combinations of vowel phonemes as peaks
permissible combinations of consonant phonemes as onsets and/or codas
relative prominence of peaks (levels of stress)
types of transition from one syllable to another

Of the four listed, the second is reserved for Chapter 5; the others are discussed below.

4.2. ITALIAN AND ENGLISH SYLLABLE PEAKS

In our discussion of vowels in English, we spoke of simple and complex vowel nuclei. Of the latter type, English /ay/, /aw/, and /oy/ could not be matched with phonetically similar vowels in Italian, because Italian has certain SEQUENCES of vowels which are closer phonetically to these English nuclei. The Italian two-vowel sequences are called DIPHTHONGS. Both vowels of a diphthong occur in the same syllable peak; phonetically, one of them has a semi-vowel positional variant.

In Italian, only /u/ and /i/ function as the semi-vowel members of diphthongs. They may occur either before or after the full vowel members. Altogether there are twenty-one diphthongs in Italian.

Six with /i/ first:

/ie/: insieme, pietà
/iɛ/: chiesa
/ia/: chiamare
/iɔ/: chiodo
/io/: piombo
/iu/: fiume

Six with /u/ first:

/ui/: quì
/ue/: questo
/uɛ/: quercia
/ua/: quando, uguale
/uɔ/: uomo, nuovo
/uo/: quotalizio, nuotare

Six with /i/ after:

/ei/: pei (per i)
/ɛi/: sei
/ai/: mai
/ɔi/: poi, eroico
/oi/: voi
/ui/: lùi

Three with /u/ after:

/eu/: eufonia
/ɛu/: euro
/au/: laurea, cauto

Diphthongs may occur in Italian in syllable peaks either with or without the predominant stress (see discussion on stress below). The fact is, though, that diphthongs do occur more frequently in stressed syllable peaks than in unstressed ones. Stress prominence must not be confused with the type of prominence a full vowel has relative to a semi-vowel.

Of all the diphthongs listed, the last three are the rarest in occurrence, with /au/ occurring more often than /eu/ and /ɛu/.

All other sequences of two vowels in Italian are to be considered as constituting separate syllable peaks—for example, /ii/, /ɔe/, /ao/, /ɛa/, /ae/, as in zii, eroe, Paolo, etopea, gaettone, which are syllabically zi-i, e-ro-e, Pa-o-lo, e-to-pe-a, ga-et-to-ne.

It must be kept in mind that these observations are made on the basis of the phonetic and phonemic situations of the modern spoken language. In poetry, opera librettos, and other artistic uses of the language, any sequence of two (or more) vowels may constitute a single syllable peak. This is possible, of course, because there exist no phonemic contrasts between vowel sequences and diphthongs; the differences are entirely phonetic.

4.3. COMPARING ITALIAN DIPHTHONGS WITH ENGLISH PHONEME SEQUENCES

Phonetically, the semi-vowel at the end of an Italian diphthong has more prominence than the off glide of an English vowel nucleus—that is, the /i/ of /oi/ in Italian voi is more prominent than the /y/ of /oy/ in English boy; the /u/ of /au/ in Italian causa is more prominent than the /w/ or /aw/ in English cows. The same is true in comparing Italian /ai/ with English /ay/. This difference causes little difficulty for the English-speaking student as far as Italian /au/, /ai/, and /oi/ are concerned. Even if he does pronounce these diphthongs with a less prominent semi-vowel, there is no possibility of confusion with other phonemes. In the instance of English /ey/, however, there are two possibilities of error. The student may confuse phonetically long Italian /e/ and the diphthong /ei/, pronouncing both of them /ey/. The seriousness is increased by the failure to make a distinction between /ei/ and /ɛi/ in Italian. This failure is common among students, because English has only /ey/ to equate with Italian /ei/ and /ɛi/.

Comparing the diphthongs in Italian with the most similar phoneme sequences in English, we obtain the following results:

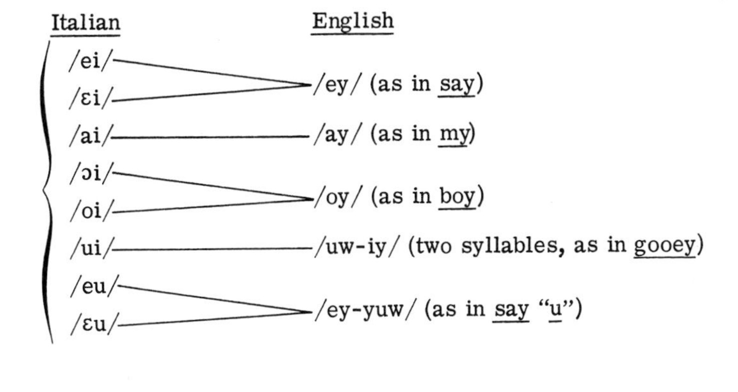

	Italian	English
semi-vowel first	/au/	/aw/ (as in loud)
	/ie/	/yey/ (as in Yates)
	/iɛ/	/ye/ (as in yet)
	/ia/	/ya/ (as in yacht)
	/iɔ/	/yo/ (as in yawl)
	/io/	/yow/ (as in yoke)
	/iu/	/yuw/ (as in few)
	/ue/	/wey/ (as in way)
	/uɛ/	/we/ (as in wet)
	/ua/	/wa/ (as in watt)
	/uɔ/	/wo/ (as in wall)
	/uo/	/wow/ (as in quote)
	/ui/	/wiy/ (as in we)

Substitution errors of English /oy/ for Italian /ɔi/ and /oi/ are parallel to the substitution of English /ey/ for /ɛi/ and /ei/ discussed above. The same is true for Italian /eu/ and /ɛu/—that is, there is one sequence in English which corresponds to two Italian diphthongs. In the Italian /ui/, /eu/ and /ɛu/, the corresponding English sequence involves two separate syllables, each containing an off glide. Consequently, the English-speaking student tends to reproduce this off glide in attempting to pronounce these diphthongs. It is well to mention here that he also tends to insert a /y/ or /w/ in making the transition between vowels when they belong to separate syllables: /y/, usually if one of the vowels is /i/, /e/, or /ɛ/, as in trattoria, maestro, etopea; /w/, if one of the vowels is /o/, /ɔ/, or /u/, as in Paolo, eroe, sua.

In the Italian diphthongs which begin with the semi-vowel, the English correspondences begin with the consonantal /y/ and /w/. The transference of English /y/ and /w/ in this instance is permissible because the Italian /i/ and /u/ have consonantal variants in this position and a similar phonetic effect is achieved.

4.4. ITALIAN TRIPHTHONGS

A triphthong is a sequence of three vowel phonemes, one a full vowel and two semi-vowels, which occur in the same syllable peak. There are only five triphthongs which occur commonly in Italian:

/iɛi/, as in miei

/uei/, as in quei

/uai/, as in guai

/uɔi/, as in buoi, puoi

/uoi/, as in the first syllable of cuoiaio (cuoi-ai-o)

Phonetically similar sequences of phonemes can be found in English for three of the five:

/yey/, as in yea (similar to Italian /iεi/)

/wey/, as in way (similar to Italian /uei/)

/way/, as in wye (similar to Italian /uai/)

Just as with sequences similar to the Italian diphthongs, the student may transfer his pronunciation of the three sequences above with fairly satisfactory results. Of course, special attention should be given to the off glide. The English-speaking student will have the same tendency not to give it enough prominence in Italian.

Phonetically similar sequences in English to correspond with Italian /uoi/ and /uɔi/ can be found only in rare instances (e.g., in quoits). Consequently, words like puoi and buoi will necessitate extra drill, since they involve unfamiliar phoneme sequences. A commonly observed tendency is to give such words two syllables (pu-oi, bu-oi), so as to use a sequence of two familiar vowel nuclei /uw/ and /oy/.

4.5. SYLLABIFICATION OF VOWEL SEQUENCES

In words which contain the vowel sequences /aio/, /ɔio/, /oio/, and the like, there may be some confusion about syllable division. Does /i/ belong to the first of the two peaks or to the second? It belongs to the first peak, as in fer-rai-o, cuoi-o, cal-zo-lai-o, since in this environment the /i/ has the phonetic characteristics of its post-vocalic variant. If it belonged to the second peak, it would of course have the phonetic quality of its prevocalic variant. Thus words like ferraio must be pronounced with the diphthong /ai/ plus final /o/, rather than with the vowel /a/ plus diphthong /io/.

More about transition from syllable to syllable is given below under Juncture (¶4.8).

4.6. /i/IN CONSONANTAL ENVIRONMENTS

In somewhat older Italian, /i/ functioned as a type of support vowel, separating some sequences of consonants, as in in ispirito, per istrada, con isdegno. Today, Italian maintains this pattern feature in only a few set phrases and with the names of countries beginning with /s/ plus another consonant, when they follow the preposition in: in Ispagna, in Isvizzera, and so on. It should be pointed out to the student that this is no longer obligatory in the general patterning of Italian pronunciation. In a few such instances, a short explanation of the older situation may be useful and valid in facilitating the teaching of a modern irregularity.

4.7. STRESS AND OTHER SIMULTANEOUS PHONEMES

In Chapter 2, pairs of words were given to illustrate the presence in both English and Italian of phonemic stress. What was not shown is that both languages have different levels of stress and different arrangements of stresses. Italian is usually taught to Americans as having only two levels of stress: one syllable (or vowel) is simply stressed or unstressed. In a word that contains only two syllables, there can of course be only two levels of stress. There, however, are utterances in Italian which show a level of stress intermediate between the two illustrated in *canto* and *cantò*. *Stuzzicadenti*, for example, has its strongest stress on the penultimate syllable. The remaining syllables are, however, not of equal prominence, the first being more strongly stressed than the other three. Moreover, one cannot predict the occurrence of this intermediate level of stress, since it occurs in other places in such words as *asciugamano* and *finalmente*, and is absent in words such as *dolomite* and *opportunità*. A good example of this contrast in stress levels is found in comparing the utterances *portabagagli* (*baggage carrier*) and *porta bagagli* (*he carries baggage*). The stress on the first syllable of *porta* in the word for *baggage carrier* is clearly not as prominent as the stress on the first syllable of the verb form. We must forget for the moment that *porta bagagli* is two words and *portabagagli* is one; as we shall see in our discussion on juncture below, there is no difference in transition between syllables and words in Italian. The written spaces are purely grammatical boundaries never heard in the spoken language.

There is yet another degree of stress which occurs in conjunction with intonation—a degree of loudness greater than that of the second syllable of *bagagli* is found in the analysis of normal conversation. It is a movable stress which is used to form what is called the CENTER of the intonation and the position of greatest emphasis in an utterance. For example, the utterance *Mio figlio è andato a Napoli* can be said with added emphasis on any of its segments. If the speaker wishes to emphasize *figlio*, he puts the greatest degree of stress on that word instead of its normal stress, and so on.

We shall indicate the different degrees of stress with the following symbols: /˝/, the most prominent or highest degree, which will be discussed further in Chapter 6 along with intonation; /´/, the strongest word stress; /`/, the intermediate word stress; /˘/, the weakest degree of stress. The last-mentioned is also conveniently referred to as "no stress," and syllables bearing it are often designated as "unstressed." Consequently it remains unmarked in the citing of examples. The symbol /˘/ is used only in discussing it separately. Examples with stress symbols added are pòrtabagágli, asciùgamáno, dòlce-méente.

The comparison of English and Italian stress patterns will be presented in ¶4.9, below. There are two other simultaneous phonemes which function strictly as part of intonation in both English and Italian: PITCH and TERMINAL CONTOUR. Pitch in human speech is not absolute like musical pitch; voice pitch is relative, and depends on each individual. The differences between each pitch level in language must therefore be relative to the key that the speaker naturally uses. For example, a man with a deep voice and a woman with a high voice may say the expression Come here! each using his own high pitch. Actually, although the deeper voice of the man will make his high pitch level much lower than the woman's, both will be understood as having spoken with high pitches. As speakers of English, both have four distinct levels of pitch which are keyed to the natural timbre of that individual's voice.

Pitch will be discussed more fully in Chapter 6. The important point to recognize here is that, in Italian or in English, pitches do not change the lexical meanings of individual words the way degrees of stress can. Instead, pitch and the rest of intonation serve as a kind of running comment on what is being said; it gives, as it were, another dimension of meaning to the utterance. One may say the name John with such variation in intonation as to convey the added meaning of anger, questioning, admiration, remorse, affection, and so on.

A terminal contour—that is, the manner in which an intonation comes to an end as the speaker reaches a pause—may consist of either a rise in pitch, or a fall, or neither. The meaning conveyed by a terminal contour is of the same type as that conveyed by pitch. Further discussion of the kinds of terminal contour, and the symbols used to indicate the various contours and pitch levels, is included in Chapter 6.

4.8. JUNCTURE

The term JUNCTURE describes the ways in which speech segments are connected. In other words, juncture defines the kinds of transition between sounds in a language. In Italian, there is only one contrast of juncture: CLOSE versus OPEN. Close juncture is the kind of transition a native speaker of Italian makes as he passes from syllable to syllable and from word to word. It is important to remember that in Italian there is no difference in transition between word units and syllable units. As mentioned above, the spaces left on the sheet of paper in writing Italian are markers of a different kind of unit. Compare the transition between the syllables of the word affatto with that between the separate words of the expression ha fatto (which in standard Italian is /affátto/ with /ff/;

see Chapter 5 for double consonants). If you say them in a normal way to another person, he will hear no difference. Open juncture, on the other hand, is the kind of audible pause that comes at the end of a breath group after a terminal contour. In normal conversation, the speaker of Italian uses open junctures only at the ends of utterances, though he may occasionally use it to emphasize either syllable or word divisions as in spelling (a-f-f-a-t-t-o), or in counting (uno-due-tre-quattro-etc.).

English has both open and close juncture and an additional phoneme called DISJUNCTURE. Whereas Italian has only one type of transition between sounds within an utterance, English has two. English disjuncture manifests itself in many ways, but its presence is always felt. Compare the difference in transition between the first two words of a nice man and an ice man, or between it sprays and it's praise, stop spinning and stops pinning, buy cakes and bike aches. Disjuncture may also occur inside a word in English—for example, in slyness, where it is characterized by a greater length of vowel nucleus than is heard in a similar word without disjuncture, such as minus.

The English-speaking student is therefore likely to transfer into Italian this added element of disjuncture. He will do it especially in reading aloud or in composing original utterances in recitation. Between two stressed vowels, disjuncture is likely to turn up in the form of a lengthened first vowel; compare Italian Chi è? with English key "a." Consonants may turn up in the coda of a preceding syllable rather than in the onset of the proper syllable—for example, un-uomo, sant-Antonio. Doubtless the only way to combat this sort of error is to give the student an early awareness of differences in juncture. Subsequent drill on speaking in breath groups will then be meaningful.

4.9. THE STRESS PATTERNS OF ITALIAN AND ENGLISH WORDS

Although both English and Italian have four degrees of stress, the similarity in patterning is minimal. The highest degree /˝/ is part of intonation in both, but the patterning of all four is different.

According to stress patterns, there are five types of words in Italian:

1. Words with strong stress (/´/) on the last syllable. They may have as few as one and as many as five syllables. All other syllables are unstressed (/˘/).

Words of one syllable: puó, dái, trám, spórt, fílm

Words of two syllables: cittá, cantó, saró

Words of three syllables: caritá, ritornó, canteró, indicó

Words of four syllables: complicitá, abilitá

Words of five syllables: opportunitá

Of Type 1, the two- and three-syllable words are the most common in occurrence.

2. Words with /´/ on the penultimate syllable and /˘/ on the last. The number of unstressed syllables preceding the one with /´/ is not relevant. Some examples are: cánto, víta, amóre, mangiáre, dolomíte. Words of this type are by far the most common in Italian.

3. Words containing /´/ followed by more than one unstressed syllable. As in type 2, the number of unstressed syllables preceding /´/ is not relevant.

/´/ followed by two /˘/s: cántano, vívere, úndici, ritornárono
/´/ followed by three /˘/s: índicano, s'accómodino
/´/ followed by four /˘/s: índicagliene

4. Words containing an intermediate stress (/`/). The intermediate stress is always on a syllable preceding the strong stress, and is always separated by at least one unstressed syllable. There are four subtypes depending on how many unstressed syllables separate the one with /`/ from the one with /´/:

separated by one: làvamáno, lùstrascárpe, pòrtacénere
separated by two: pòrtabagágli, pòrtavivánde
separated by three: còntrovelaccíno
separated by four: càcciatorpediniéra

Of the four subtypes, the first two are the most common in occurrence. The last two occur rarely.

5. Words which normally occur in a sentence without primary stress. There are three subtypes:

words with /˘/ only: su, in, da, il, la, un, con
words with /`/ followed by /˘/: còntro, nègli, dèlle, ùna
words with /˘/ before /`/ : perchè (with the meaning because).

Words of this type are mostly articles, prepositions, and conjunctions.

A comparison with English stress patterns is tabulated below:

Italian Pattern	Italian Example	Closest English Equivalent	Transference Acceptable
´	trám	trám	yes
˘ ´	cittá	insíśt, còmpáct	perhaps

Italian Pattern	Italian Example	Closest English Equivalent	Transference Acceptable
◡◡´	canteró	ùnawáre, unawáre	perhaps
◡◡◡ ´	ritorneró	înterreláte	no
◡◡◡◡ ´	opportunitá	pròcommunístic	no
´◡	cánto	cánon, pérmît	perhaps
◡´◡	insíste	insístant	yes
◡◡ ´◡	dolomíte	àutomátic, automátic	perhaps
´◡◡	fécero	éffigy, résumè	perhaps
◡´◡◡	ritórnano	belátedly	yes
◡◡´◡◡	dolomítico	phònológical	no
´◡◡◡	índicano	ínsolently, cápitalîze	perhaps
´◡◡◡◡	índicagliene	nátionalîsm	no
`◡´◡	làvamáno	àutomátic, automátic	perhaps
`◡◡´◡	pòrtabagágli	pròcommunístic	yes
`◡◡◡´◡	còntrovelaccíno	còunterrèformátion	no
`◡◡◡◡´◡	càcciatorpediniéra	indùstrializátion	no
◡	a (preposition)	at (e.g., at home)	yes
` ◡	dòpo	âfter	yes
◡`	perchè (because)	becàuse	yes

The first column gives the Italian pattern with stresses indicated. The second column contains an example in Italian. The third contains examples taken from English which are the most similar to the Italian pattern. In the fourth column, we have indicated wheth or not the English pattern is sufficiently like the Italian pattern to be transferred effectively. There are some conditional transfers which we have indicated with the word "perhaps."

Most instances of unacceptable transference are due to the presence of an intermediate stress in the English equivalent where Italian has a weak stress. As a result, the English-speaking student is likely to transfer the stress pattern of the English word nátionalîsm in attempting to say the Italian word índicagliene, thereby saying something like índicagliène; for dolomíte, he may say dòlomíte, and so on. All Italian words contain ing intermediate stress, excluding those like còntrovelaccíno and càcciatorpediniéra whic are rare anyway, have stress patterns paralleling English types. The opposite is not true English has many more patterns containing intermediate stress than does Italian. The four conditionally acceptable transfers (indicated by "perhaps") are instances in which speakers of English vary between using a weak and an intermediate stress where Italian has only weak stress. Consequently, the teacher will find some of the students having no trouble using the correct stress pattern on words like cánto, fécero, and cantó, whereas others will be saying cántò, fécerò, càntó.

Training the student to use proper stress patterns in speaking Italian is one of the most difficult tasks a teacher faces. First of all, the student is usually unaware that his own language contains three degrees of word stress. Second, the orthography of Italian allows for the marking of strong stress only when it occurs on the last syllable of a word. As a result, the student may persist in stress errors long after he has mastered many of the other new sound patterns. In explaining and illustrating differences in stress, it is advisable to concentrate early on those Italian patterns in which the learner is likely to introduce /ˋ/ wrongly.

4.10. VOWEL ALTERNATION

One type of vowel patterning in Italian is conditioned primarily by changes in stress and also partly by consonant environment. We observe an alternation of two sets of vowels: /e/ alternates with /ɛ/, and /o/ alternates with /ɔ/. Each member of both sets occurs before all consonants in syllables bearing a strong stress (/ˊ/) or an intermediate stress (/ˋ/). In unstressed syllables, only the second member of both sets (/ɛ/, /ɔ/) can be found before the consonants /m/, /n/, /ɲ/, /l/, /ʎ/, /r/. Conversely, only the first member of both sets (/e/, /o/) occurs before all other consonants under the same conditions of stress. If it were not for the environment under stress, /e/ and /ɛ/, /o/ and /ɔ/ would not be separate phonemes. To illustrate how this alternation operates, let us note the following sets of words:

/é/ is replaced by /ɛ/: momento /moménto/, but momentino /mɔmɛntíno/, regno /réɲɲo/, but regnare /rɛɲɲáre/, capello /kapéllo/, but capellino /kapɛllíno/, sera /séra/ but serata /sɛráta/

/ó/ is replaced by /ɔ/: secondo /sekóndo/, but secondario /sekɔndário/, rompere /rómpɛre/, but rompiamo /rɔmpiámo/, bisogno /bisóɲɲo/, but bisognoso /bisɔɲɲóso/

Before these same consonants, /ɛ/ and /ɔ/ remain unchanged: presenta /presɛ́nta/ and presentare /presɛntáre/, bene /bɛ́ne/ and benedetto /bɛnedétto/, domino /dɔ́mino/ and dominare /dɔmináre/, corpo /kɔ́rpo/ and corporale /kɔrpɔrále/.

Before all other consonants, with the same shift in stress:

/έ/ is replaced by /e/: sette /sέtte/, but settimana /settimána/, reggere /rέǧǧεre/, but reggiamo /reǧǧámo/, feudo /fέudo/, but feudale /feudále/

/ɔ́/ is replaced by /o/: lotta /lɔ́tta/, but lottare /lottáre/, povero /pɔ́vεro/, but poveretto /povεrétto/, poco /pɔ́ko/ but pochino /pokíno/

/e/ and /o/ remain unchanged: secco /sékko/ and seccare /sekkáre/, soffio /sóffio/ and soffiare /soffiáre/

In this alternation of vowels we find another illustration of our earlier statement that control of the pronunciation of individual sounds is not enough. The student must be equally aware of the **PATTERNS** in which each occurs.

Perhaps some of the shock of discovering that such a pattern of vowels exist in Italian can be lessened if it is pointed out that English too has vowel alternation of a much more involved nature. Let us note, for example, the various vowel shifts in the following pairs:

politics but political
athlete but athletic
reproduce but reproduction
atom but atomic
repeat but repetition

4.11. STRESS LEVELS AND RELATIVE SYLLABLE PROMINENCE

In English, all vowels in unstressed syllables tend to be short and (at least to an Italian ear) indistinct. By compensation, syllables bearing either a strong or an intermediate stress are of longer **DURATION** than those with no stress. This situation does not exist in Italian. Regardless of degree of stress, each syllable is of approximately equal duration. The only vowel alternation caused by stress is the one described above. The student who transfers his English habit of reducing the duration of unstressed syllables (or even dropping some altogether, as in int'ressante) is not reproducing the timing of Italian correctly.

COMPARING CONSONANT PATTERNS 5

5.0.

Vowel and stress patterns were discussed together in the last chapter, because the vowels of both languages are affected by changes in stress, as we demonstrated. On the other hand, consonant patterning in both is unaffected by changes in stress. The following discussion will show that the learner's chief difficulties with consonants arise from unfamiliar sequences. Contrary to popular belief, Italian is not a language which contains fewer groups of consonants per syllable than English and which is therefore "easier to pronounce." The difference between the two languages is to be found more in the locations of consonant sequences and in the kinds of consonants that occur in these sequences. Whereas words like cuoiaio present a problem in vowel patterning, words like sgelare and sradicare offer equally great difficulty in consonant patterning.

The method of comparison remains essentially that used in the previous chapters. Italian consonant patterning is described first, then matched with English. Problems caused by divergency in pattern are thereby recognized and diagnosed.

5.1. THE SYLLABLE AND THE CONSONANT

Again the syllable forms the framework of our discussion. Problems in consonant patterning occur either in the margins of one syllable or across the margins of adjoining syllables. As pointed out in Chapter 4, there are two syllable margins: the onset, preceding the peak; and the coda following it. All the consonants of Italian may occur singly in the onset. Only two, /ɲ/ and /ʎ/, are markedly infrequent in this occurrence. Of the two, more examples can be found with /ɲ/ as onset than with /ʎ/—for example, gnaulo, gnocco. On the other hand, /ʎ/ may occur more often in any given stretch of Italian. This is because of its occurrence as onset in the frequent form gli.

Occurrence of single consonants in syllable codas depends on the position of the syllable. If it is the last in the word (word-final), three consonants are frequently found in the coda: /l/, /r/, /n/—for example, il (al, del, and its other combinations with prepositions), quel, bel, per, in, con. Word-final /s/, /t/, and some others turn up in foreign loans and neologisms such as lapis, fiat, sud. Widespread in older Italian and still prevalent in the formal language (and literature) of today is a phenomenon called APOCOPATION, or the dropping of final vowels. However, even with this taken into consideration the resulting word-final consonant is usually /l/, /r/ or /n/ and /m/, as in amabil, ancor dar, cantan, andiam.

If we included in this analysis the words which have been borrowed recently from French, German, and English, we could find examples of every consonant except /ɲ/ and /ʎ/ occurring in the codas of word-final syllables. We do not include these foreign borrowings, however, since most of them have not yet acquired permanent status in the vocabulary or uniform pronunciation throughout the Italian peninsula.

The occurrence of single consonants in the codas of syllables not in word-final position is discussed below.

5.2. CONSONANT SEQUENCES IN ITALIAN

Within the onset margin of one syllable, sequences of two and three consonants are permissible. There are longer sequences, but they are found only across syllable boundaries—for example, per strapazzare /perstrapaccáre/. No consonant sequences occur in a syllable coda, except at the end of a few of the borrowed words referred to above (e.g., sport, nord, film).

All possible sequences of two consonants in Italian are indicated in the following tabulation:

	p	b	t	d	k	g	f	v	s	š	c	z	č	ǧ	m	n	ɲ	l	ʎ	r
p	O								ⓧ							ⓧ		ⓧ		ⓧ
b		O		O					O							O		ⓧ		ⓧ
t			O												ⓧ	O		ⓧ		ⓧ
d				O		O									O					ⓧ
k			O		O				O						O	O		ⓧ		ⓧ
g				O		O									O			ⓧ		ⓧ
f				O			O											ⓧ		ⓧ
v								O												O
s	ⓧ	ⓧ	ⓧ	ⓧ	ⓧ	ⓧ	ⓧ	ⓧ	O					ⓧ	ⓧ	ⓧ	X	ⓧ		ⓧ
š										O										
c											O									

	p	b	t	d	k	g	f	v	s	š	c	ʒ	č	ǧ	m	n	ɲ	l	ʎ	r
ʒ												O								
č													O							
ǧ														O						
m	O	O													O	(X)		O		
n			O	O	O	O	O	O	O	O	O	O	O	O		O		O		O
ɲ																	O			
l	O	O	O	O	O	O	O	O	O		O	O	O	O	O	O		O		O
ʎ																			O	
r	O	O	O	O	O	O	O	O	O	O	O	O	O	O	O	O	O	O	O	O

Key

O - occurrence only across syllable boundaries

X - occurrence only within the onset of one syllable

(X) - occurrence in both environments

The first consonant in the sequence is found in the left-hand column. The second consonant of the sequence is listed in the row across the top. The key given below the table indicates whether the sequence occurs across syllable boundaries, within the onset of one syllable, or in both positions. In those sequences occurring across syllable boundaries, the first consonant is in the coda of a preceding syllable and the second in the onset of a following one. In this way, the chart covers all occurrences of single consonants in syllable codas which were not discussed in ¶ 5.1. The following are examples of sequences of two consonants:

Double Consonant Sequences

pp: grappa
bb: babbo
tt : tutto
dd: addio
kk: acca
gg: agguato
ff : affatto
vv: ovvio
ss: passo
šš: uscio

cc : pazzo
ʒʒ : mezzo
čč : minaccia
ǧǧ : coraggio
mm: mamma
nn : anno
ɲɲ : legno
ll : stella
ʎʎ : figlio
rr : terra

Sequences of Dissimilar Consonants

*ps : psichiatra, apepsia
*pn : pneumatico, ipnotico
pl : plastico, duplicare
pr : provato represso
*bd : abdicare
*bs : abside
*bn : abnegare
bl : blocco, Dublino
br : braccio, ubriaco
*tm : tmesi, atmosfera
*tn : etnico
*tl : tlissi, atletico
tr : tratta, ritratto
dg : Edgardo
*dm : cadmio
dr : dragone, quadro
*kt : factoturn
*ks : uxoricidio
*km : acme
*kn : acne
kl : classe, declinare
kr : critica, microfono
*gd : Bagdad
*gm : pragmatico
gl : glicine, negligenza
gr : grande, segregare
*fd : Afdera
fl : flotta, riflesso
fr : frase, refrazione
vr : avrei
sp : spesso, aspettare
sb : sbaglio, disborso
st : stesso, masticare
sd : sdegno, posdomani
sk : scacciare, maschera
sg : sgonfiato, disgusto
sf : sfumare, fosforo
sv : svanire, risveglio
sǧ : sgelare, disgiunto
sm : smarrire, dismantare
sn : snello, disnodare
*sɲ : sgnaulio
sl : slavo, dislogare
sr : sregolato, disradicare
mp : impallidire
mb : imbecille
*mn : mnemonico, amnistia
ml : Amleto
nt : antico
nd : indietro
nk : incontro
ng : unghia
nf : tonfo
nv : inverno
ns : pensare
nš : inscindibile
nc : senza
nʐ : ronzare
nč : cominciare
nǧ : ungere
nl : in lista
*nr : sanrocchino
lp : calpestato
lb : alba
lt : volta
ld : falda

---

*designates a sequence of low frequency found in technical, learned, or rare words.

lk :	calcagno	rb :	arboscello	rm :	marmo
lg :	amalgama	rt :	parte	rn :	perno
lf :	alfabeta	rd :	dardo	rɲ :	per gnaulare
lv :	alveolare	rk :	marca	rl :	perla
ls :	malsano	rg :	organico	rʎ :	per gli studi
lc :	calza	rf :	orfano		
lz̨ :	belzebú	rv :	orvieto		
lč :	calcio	rs :	perso		
lǧ :	belgio	rš :	per sciaguattare		
lm :	calma	rc :	scherzo		
ln :	malnoto	rz̨ :	garza		
lr :	Ulrico	rč :	marcia		
rp :	sterpo	rǧ :	argento		

/r/ is the only consonant which may be followed by any other consonant, including itself. But there are also no onset sequences with /r/ as first member; such sequences occur only across syllable boundaries, as do those beginning with /l/ and /n/. /s/ has a high frequency of occurrence as the first member of consonant sequences both across syllable boundaries and in syllable onsets. The latter distribution is mostly due to the fact that the phoneme /s/ represents a grammatically significant prefix _s-_, as in _sgelare_, _sfumare_. The proper pronunciation of /s/-initial sequences thus takes on special importance.

5.2.1. VARIATIONS IN CONSONANT SEQUENCES

Four rare sequences of dissimilar consonants are often replaced by double consonants. The first member of the sequence is replaced by a double of the second member. This process is known as ASSIMILATION—that is, the first consonant assimilates to the second. The four sequences affected are /bd/, /bn/, /ks/ and /gm/.

/bd/ becomes /dd/—for example, _abdicare_ becomes /addicáre/
/bn/ becomes /nn/—for example, _abnorme_ becomes /annɔ́rme/
/ks/ becomes /ss/—for example, _uxoricidio_ becomes /ussɔričídio/
/gm/ becomes /mm/—for example, _pragmatico_ becomes /prammátiko/

The four assimilations listed above are optional, but three replacements of /n/ are obligatory. Standard Italian does not have the sequences /nm/, /np/, and /nb/. In these instances, /n/ is replaced by /m/, as in

San Marco pronounced /sammárko/ (/mm/)

un poco pronounced /umpɔ́ko/ (/mp/)

in bocca pronounced /imbókka/ (/mb/)

When the sequence involves a grammatical word boundary, as in the examples above, the letter n is retained in the spelling. If, however, the sequence occurs in what is officially one word, m is usually written—for example, sampiero, sampietrini, imboccare.

5.2.2. DOUBLE CONSONANT SEQUENCES

Perhaps the outstanding feature of consonant patterning in Italian is the occurrence of double consonants. The diagonal line on the chart, above, well illustrates two important aspects of their distribution: all consonants in Italian may occur doubled; sequences of double consonants occur only across syllable boundaries—for example, grap-p tut-to, ad-dio. (A phonetic doubling of onset consonants is connected with a type of intonation. See Chapter 6.)

The chief phonetic feature of double-consonant sequences is length. In stops and fricatives, the position of articulation is held one and one half to two times as long as with single consonants before being released. Double /rr/ is pronounced by flapping the tongue tip several times against the alveolar ridge instead of just once. Articulation of double continuants is simply twice as long as that of single continuants.

From a strictly phonetic viewpoint, there are no double consonants in Italian except /rr/. We say this because pronunciation of the sequences described above does not involve two completely separate articulations but rather the holding of a single articulation. The term "double consonant" describes an arrangement of phonemes in Italian which is distinct from the phonetic realization of such an arrangement. This point will take on added importance (and become clearer) later in the present chapter when the comparison with English is made.

Three consonants occur only in double sequences within a word: /š/, /ɲ/, and /ʎ/—that is, no pairs of words contrast only because of a difference between /š/ and /šš/ /ɲ/ and /ɲɲ/, /ʎ/ and /ʎʎ/ in their interiors. It is often difficult to convince even native Italians of this fact, since the writing system does not account for the doubling of these consonants (cf. figlio, lascio, bagna). Yet phonetic evidence proves that gn, for example, represents a longer sound in a word like bagno than it does in a word like gnocco, and that the sound represented by sci in lascio is definitely longer than the initial sound of the word sciame. Even more convincing is the fact that the consonant sequence within bagno is as long as that within danno, and that both have short vowels phonetically.

5.2.3. SYNTACTIC DOUBLING

For most speakers of the standard language in central and southern Italy, all initial consonants are consistently doubled after some words (e, é, da, a, che, and so on). This phenomenon is termed SYNTACTIC DOUBLING; it is only partly indicated by the writing system—for example, /dakkápo/ (daccapo or da capo), /dakké/ (dacché or da che), /ekkóme/ (eccome or e come).

In other instances it is almost never indicated: /perkésseivenúto/ (perché sei venuto), /kosíffánnotútte/ (cosí fanno tutte), /akkavállo/ (a cavallo).

Although, particularly in the north, standard Italian is spoken natively with syntactic doubling only where indicated by the writing system, it is well to explain full syntactic doubling to students, since there are speakers who regularly practice it. Our textbooks generally fail even to mention it.

5.3. SEQUENCES OF THREE CONSONANTS

At the beginning of ¶ 5.2 we stated that sequences of three consonants may occur in the syllable onset in Italian. Actually there are just ten possible sequences of three consonants in syllable onsets, each beginning with /s/ and ending with either /r/ or /l/. The number of three-consonant sequences occurring across syllable boundaries raises the total to twenty-nine, tabulated as follows:

	k	g	p	b	t	d	f
r	r,l	r	r		r		
l	l				r		r
m			r,l	r,l			
n	r	r,l			r	r	r,l
s	r,l	r,l	r,l	r,l	r	r	r

The consonants listed in the left-hand column are the first members; those across the top are the second members; the third members are noted in the corresponding boxes. All sequences except those beginning with /s/ occur only across a syllable boundary. The boundary is after the first member—for example, /r-kr/ in ipercritico. Sequences beginning with /s/ may occur either across syllable boundaries or in onset position. Examples are as follows:

rkr : ipercritico
rkl : intercludere
rgr : burgravio
rpr : sorprendere
rtr : artritico
lkl : folclore
ltr : altro
lfr : Alfredo
mpr : comprendere
mpl : semplice
mbr : ombra
mbl : emblema
nkr : cancro
ngr : ingrassare
ngl : inglese

ntr : scontro
ndr : scafandro
nfl : conflitto
nfr : cianfruglione
skr : scrivere, ascrivere
skl : sclerite, esclamare
sgr : sgridare, disgraziato
spr : sprigionare, aspro
spl : splendore, risplendere
sbr : sbraciare, disbrigare
sbl : sbloccare
str : stregato, lastra
sdr : sdraio
sfr : sfruttare, disfrenare
*sgl : sglutinare

5.4. SUMMARY OF CONSONANT PATTERNING IN ITALIAN

The following general statements can be made about the arrangements of consonants in Italian.

All consonants occur singly in syllable onsets.

The occurrence of single consonants in syllable codas is highly restricted in comparison with that in onset position.

Italian has sequences of two and three consonants in syllable onsets, but normally not in syllable codas.

Many more sequences of two and three consonants occur across syllable bound aries than in syllable onsets.

All consonants occur double, across syllable boundaries only.

/š/, /ɲ/, and /ʎ/ occur only double with a word.

Double consonants are a feature of phoneme patterning.

5.5. COMPARISON WITH ENGLISH

The patterns of English consonants will be discussed only insofar as they diffe from those of Italian and therefore cause the learner difficulty.

5.5.1 SINGLE CONSONANTS

The onset occurrence of the following four Italian consonants is unmatched in English: /c/, /ʐ/, /ɲ/, /ʎ/. As we pointed out earlier (Chapter 3), /c/ and /ʐ/ are simila phonetically to the English sequences /ts/ and /dz/. Neither of the English sequences, however, occurs in the syllable onset position. Consequently, words like pazzo and mezzo will cause the student little or no trouble, since he can equate the medial consonants with the medial sequences of English words like Patsy and sudsy (excluding for the moment the problem of double consonants). On the other hand, he may have difficulty with the initial consonants of words like zio and zelo. He will probably tend to substitute English /s/ for Italian /c/ and English /z/ for Italian /z̧/. If he is influenced by English spelling, he may substitute English /z/ in both instances. The problem with initial /ɲ/ and /ʎ/ cannot be approached through a comparison with English, since similar phonemes do not exist in English (cf. ¶ 3.2). Theoretically, however, if the student learns how to control the articulation of these two new phonemes, he should have no greater difficulty producing them initially than elsewhere. Other occurrences of single consonants in Italian offer no particular problem in patterning to the English-speaking student.

5.5.2 SEQUENCES OF TWO CONSONANTS

There are ten sequences of dissimilar consonants in Italian which present problems for the English-speaking student: /sb/, /sd/, /sg/, /sv/, /sǧ/, /sm/, /sn/, /sɲ/, /sl/, /sr/. Observe that all have /s/ as the first member. Another similarity shared by all is that the second member in each sequence is a voiced consonant. In discussing the positional variants of /s/ in Italian, we mentioned that it has a voiced variant, [z], which occurs before voiced consonants. Therefore each sequence listed here is phonetically [z] plus voiced consonant. It is not difficult to find occurrences of /zd/, /zg/, and most of the others across syllable boundaries in English, for example, Lisbon, Tuesday, Kresge, dismal, Fresno, muslin, Israel. At least one, /zd/, occurs in codas—for example, used. Despite this phonetic pairing, there are no words in English beginning with /z/ plus consonant. This difference in patterning is important because, as mentioned earlier, /s/ represents a detachable prefix which has a high frequency of occurrence in Italian. The general tendency among students is to use the voiceless /s/ phoneme when these sequences occur in the crucial onset position, and thus to make the onsets of smarrire, snello, slavo sound like those of English smile, snail, slave. In /sb/, /sd/, /sg/, two types of incorrect transfer occur: students may either insert /ə/ between the two consonants, pronouncing [zəb], [zəd], [zəg], or devoice the second consonant, changing [zb] to [sp], [zd] to [st], [zg] to [sk].

This problem has two aspects, and is somewhat similar to that of /c/ and /z̧/, discussed above. Italian sequences of /s/ plus a voiced consonant are almost identical phonetically to English sequences of /z/ plus a voiced consonant. On the other hand, the patterning of the Italian sequences is much more like that of English /s/ plus a voiced consonant. The fact that pattern similarities between languages often exert more pressure than phonetic similarities seems borne out by the transference of English /s/ plus voiced consonant, because this is the pattern that matches Italian /s/ plus voiced consonant.

Two other consonant sequences, /tr/ and /dr/, are matched by English sequences, but may cause difficulty because of English pronunciation habits. Compare the onsets of the English words *try* and *drama* with those of the Italian words *tre* and *dramma*. Not only is English /r/ never a flap here, but /t/ and /d/ before /r/ have variants unlike Italian /t/ and /d/ in this position.

Another difference in consonant patterning between the two languages is that English lacks sequences of word-internal double consonants to match those of Italian. Double consonants, however, do occur in English across word boundaries. Except for /ɲ/, /ʎ/, /r/, and the affricates /c/, /ʐ/, the double consonant sequences of Italian are matched phonetically in English whenever a sequence of words brings together two occurrences of the same phoneme, as in:

ripe pears (/pp/)
grab bags (/bb/)
wet turf (/tt/)
wide door (/dd/)
black coal (/kk/)
leg gear (/gg/)
enough film (/ff/)
live vine (/vv/)
nice seat (/ss/)
rush showing (/šš/)
some money (/mm/)
run now (/nn/)
sell limes (/ll/)

Double consonant sequences of Italian /č/ and /ǧ/ are matched in *bit chilly* (/čč/) and *bad jar* (/ǧǧ/). Phrases like *rich child* or *large jug* would not serve to exemplify Italian /čč/ and /ǧǧ/, because in English both of the affricates are fully articulated, with a disjuncture between them, whereas in Italian only the stop element of the affricate is lengthened.

No examples can be found for double sequences of /ɲ/ and /ʎ/; these consonants are unmatched in both articulation and distribution in English. Although sequences of /rr/ can be found in English (e.g., *tar road*), there is no real phonetic similarity with Italian /rr/. The Italian sequences /cc/ and /ʐʐ/ have no equivalents; the closest phonetic equivalents in English, /ts/ and /dz/, do not occur in word-initial position.

ITALIAN AND ENGLISH INTONATION 6

6.0.

Intonation is that element of human speech through which the speaker expresses his editorial attitude toward what he is saying while he is saying it. As indicated in Chapter 2, the meaning conveyed by intonation is separate from that of the units made up of vowels and consonants. This can be quickly demonstrated by the minimal-pair technique illustrated in our discussion of phonology: minimal pairs of utterances can be found to show meaning contrasts resident in the intonation alone. For example, is we try saying yes with different pitch arrangements, we will observe that various differences in total meaning are conveyed thereby: yes as a simple colorless affirmation; yes meaning go ahead, I'm listening; yes without enthusiasm; yes with doubt or reservation; and so on. In all languages, pitch arrangement—that is, intonation patterns—are just as fully systematized as are the phonological and grammatical signals, and are every bit as important in the total message. Indeed, under circumstances impairing the audibility and intelligibility of another's signals, it is his familiarity with intonation patterns which often enables the native speaker to follow what is baffling confusion to the outsider. Native-speaking listeners have of course acquired a powerful automatic reaction to another's intonation. Consequently, the use of faulty or ill-chosen intonation by a foreign speaker is at once noticed, and may have either of two results. One is simple: an intonation which is not normal in the language being spoken merely marks the speaker as a foreigner even if his vowels and consonants are excellent. In more important instances, where the two languages share like patterns with different meanings, the foreign speaker may express an unintended attitude. For example, if a person says Buon giorno with the intonation which may accompany a cheerful Good morning in English, he risks conveying the additional meaning of: Well, at long last! You're finally up!

The comparison of intonations is complicated by the fact that patterns differ not cnly between languages but also between dialects of the same language. For example, many speakers of British English use the same arrangement of pitches for questions containing an interrogative word as for questions expecting a yes or no answer; so How did you know? and Are you there? are said with the same intonation. On the other hand, most speakers of American English will use one arrangement for questions containing interrogatives, and another with yes/no questions. The intonation patterns of standard Italian differ similarly between regional and between social groups.

Somehow connected with the intonation systems, variable as they are within a given language, is another group of phenomena called VOCAL QUALIFIERS—drawl, huskiness, overloudness, abnormal pitch variation, clipped speech, and the like—which recur at the margin of linguistic structure and yet vary largely from individual to individual. A close-grained study of comparative intonation must presumably take account of vocal qualifiers as well as of dialectal variations. In the present treatment, however, we limit our investigation and discussion to: the patterns of intonation which are prevalent throughout standard Italian on the one hand and American English on the other, and a comparison of these patterns in the two languages. By prevalent patterns, we mean simply those which are normal for all native speakers and are highly recurrent in everyday conversations.

6.1. THE STRUCTURE OF INTONATION

Phonetically, the intonation of a given utterance is a constantly changing band of pitches. Electronic instruments of various types have been devised to record these variations and to interpret them in the form of spectograms or the like. They have also been effectively represented in musical notation, since they have in common with music a number of factors such as variable pitch and duration. We have chosen to interpret them in terms of simple fluctuating lines running the length of various utterances with which they may occur:

Italian Examples	English Examples
Perché?	How are you?
Perché non c'erà.	How are you?
Si.	I'm going home.

Italian Examples	English Examples
Che volevano loro?	What's his name?
Devo andare via.	Yes.
Che cosa?	Are you American?
Subito, signore.	Why?
Ho tentato.	That's all.
Vengo . . .	What?

The following features in each utterance are thereby illustrated: the point of highest pitch, the point of lowest pitch, and the relative degrees of rise and fall in pitch. Among the features not illustrated are: the point of greatest volume in each intonation, and the absolute pitch of each syllable in terms of vibrations per second. The last-mentioned varies of course from speaker to speaker, and depends on the over-all pitch of the individual voice. That is, the same intonation patterns may be reproduced by both male and female voices with the same proportions between each pitch level but with differences in key. Of the five features mentioned above, the first four have importance in the representation of the intonation pattern as a phonemic entity—that is, as an arrangement of phonemes.

In phonemic terms, the intonation of a given utterance is stated not as a continuous fluctuation of pitch but as a discrete series of POINTS, at each successive one of which the level of pitch has meaningfully changed from, or has meaningfully remained the same as, the preceding one. Every speaker's band of phonetic pitch is divisible, for Italian and English and many other languages, into four phonemic levels: LOW, MIDDLE, HIGH, and OVERHIGH. In phonemic notation, these levels are symbolized by the superscript numbers $^{1\,2\,3\,4}$ (from low up) distributed at the relevant pitch points—that is, at the onset of a given syllable or at the end of a phrase, thus:

^{2}good ^{3}morning^1 or ^{3}good ^{2}morning^2

^{1}buon ^{2}giorno^2 or ^{2}buon ^{3}giorno^3

The number of places at which phonemic pitch may occur—PITCH POINTS—in a given intonation in Italian and American English may range from two to five. There must always be at least two, in which instance they are designated as CENTER and FINAL. The center pitch point always coincides with the PHRASE STRESS (referred to in ¶ 4.7 as the highest degree of stress, marked /˝/); that is, they both fall on one and the same syllable.

In utterances in which the first syllable receives the phrase stress, the first pitch point to occur will automatically be the center, for example, English ^{3}nőthing^{1} or Italian ^{1}nie̋nte^{1}. These same examples also serve to show that the pitch at the center and final points may be on the same level or on different levels (high-low, low-low).

In utterances (and it should be remembered that this term is not synonymous with "word") where the phrase stress is not on the first syllable, a pitch point over a preceding syllable is called INITIAL, as in English ^{2}for ^{3}nőthing^{1} or Italian ^{2}per ^{1}nie̋nte^{1}. Again, the examples will show that the pitch at these points may be on a variety of levels, though in marginal cases all three may be on the same level.

A significant change in pitch may occur between the initial and the center; such a point is called PRE-CENTRAL, and may be seen in Italian ^{2}mi ^{3}chia̋mo Gio^{1}va̋nni^{1}.

In the rather rare instances where a significant pitch point occurs between the center and the final, it is called PRE-FINAL; for example, English ^{1}wőn^{3}derful^{2}.

In utterances where there is no change in meaning between initial and center or between center and final, the pre-central and pre-final pitch points are phonemically non-existent.

A further feature of the final, which must also be taken into account, is the direction of the change, if any, imparted to its level as the voice fades into silence: rising, falling, or unchanged. This direction is called the utterance's TERMINAL CONTOUR, and is represented by an arrow, as follows: ↑ rising, ↓ falling, → unchanged; Examples with English no:

^{3}nő^{2} ↓ ^{3}nő^{1} ↓ ^{3}nő^{3} ↑ ^{3}nő^{2} ↑ ^{3}nő^{3} → ^{3}nő^{2} →

A phonemic rewriting of the examples first represented phonetically above is:

Italian Examples	English Examples
^{2}Per^{1}che̋^{1} ↓	^{2}How ^{3}a̋re you^{1} ↓
^{2}Per^{3}ché non ^{1}c'e̋ra^{1} ↓	^{2}How are ^{3}yőu^{1} ↓
^{3}Sí˝^{2} ↓	^{3}I̋'m going home^{1} ↓
^{3}Ché volévano ^{1}lőro^{1} ↓	^{2}What's his ^{3}na̋me^{1} ↓
^{2}Dévo an^{3}dáre ^{1}vía̋^{1} ↓	^{3}Ye̋s^{2} ↓

Italian Examples	English Examples
^{2}Ché ^{3}cősa^{1} ↓	^{2}Are you A^{3}me̋rican^{3} ↑
^{3}Súbito^{2} → ^{2}si^{1}gnőre^{1} ↓	^{3}Why̋^{2} ↑
^{2}Ho ^{3}ten^{1}ta̋^{2}to^{1} ↓	^{2}That's ^{3}a̋ll^{2} →
^{2}Ve̋ngo^{2} ↑	^{3}Wha̋t^{3} ↑

Italian

6.2. THE BASIC PATTERNS

The two basic patterns occur with high frequency in normal everyday conversation. These two are to be considered basic in the sense that they are the "uncolored" intonations which serve merely to transmit a message (no message is transmittable without an intonation) and do not convey to the listener any editorial loading, on the part of the speaker, of that message as a whole or of any element within it. It is in the many available departures from the basic patterns that the speaker conveys, and the hearer apprehends, editorial slants.

Of the two basic ("no comment") patterns, one is used in questions expected to elicit a yes/no answer, and the other is used in other types of sentence: statements, requests, questions containing a grammatically interrogative word. In both patterns, the phrase stress and therefore also the center of the intonation is on the last syllable receiving stress; neither has a pre-final pitch point. We treat first the pattern used in sentences other than yes/no questions.

1. This pattern may be stated by the formula /. . . ^{1} ˝ ^{1} ↓/—that is, the center and the final are both low, and the terminal is falling. The ellipses in the formula indicate that certain variations are possible before the center; these are largely predictable in terms of word stresses. The variations are as follows:

No syllabic material precedes the center, as in:

/^{1} ˝ ^{1} ↓/ {
^{1}si̋^{1} ↓
^{1}pi ő ve^{1} ↓
^{1}se̋ttimo^{1} ↓

The center is preceded by one or more unstressed syllables which generate an initial middle pitch, as in:

/^{2} ^{1} ˝ ^{1} ↓/ {
^{2}da ^{1}na̋poli^{1} ↓
^{2}glielo ^{1}da̋^{1} ↓
^{2}me ne ^{1}va̋do^{1} ↓

The center is preceded by material containing one or more stressed syllables, including one at the beginning, which generates an initial high pitch, as in:

$/^{3\ 1\ ''\ 1}\downarrow/$

^{3}dévo par^{1}ti̋re^{1} $\downarrow$
^{3}questo é ^{1}ve̋ro^{1} $\downarrow$
^{3}chí ha détto ^{1}que̋sto^{1} $\downarrow$

The same as above, but with an unstressed syllable at the beginning which generates an initial middle pitch, although a subsequent stressed syllable generates a precentral high pitch, as in:

$/^{2\ 3\ 1\ ''\ 1}\downarrow/$

^{2}mi ^{3}chiámo Gio^{1}va̋nni^{1} $\downarrow$
^{2}lo cono^{3}sciámo be^{1} ni̋ssimo^{1} $\downarrow$
^{2}da ^{3}dóve ar^{1} ri̋vano^{1} $\downarrow$

If more than one stressed syllable is present, there is a choice as to where the pre-central pitch may occur:

^{2}il ^{3}fíglio si chiáma Ro^{1}dólfo^{1} $\downarrow$

but: ^{2}si chiáma Ro^{3}dólfo Settem^{1}bri̋ni^{1} $\downarrow$

2. The second pattern, used in yes/no questions, may be stated by the formula $/\ldots^{3\ ''\ 3}\uparrow/$. Here both the center and the final are high, and the terminal is rising. The variations are as follows:

No syllabic material precedes the center, as in:

$/^{3\ ''\ 3}\uparrow/$

^{3}sı̋^{3} $\uparrow$
^{3}piőve^{3} $\uparrow$
^{3}se̋ttimo^{3} $\uparrow$

Any material preceding the center, regardless of stress distributions within it, generates an initial middle pitch, as in:

$/^{2\ 3\ ''\ 3}\uparrow/$

^{2}da ^{3}Na̋poli^{3} $\uparrow$
^{2}glielo ^{3}da̋^{3} $\uparrow$
^{2}te ne ^{3}va̋i^{3} $\uparrow$
^{2}déve par^{3}ti̋re^{3} $\uparrow$
^{2}si chiáma Gio^{3}va̋nni^{3} $\uparrow$

The two basic patterns /. . . ^{1} ˝ ^{1} ↓/ and /. . . ^{3} ˝ ^{3} ↑/ stand in grammatically functional contrast in some instances where intonation alone differentiates a yes/no question from a statement or the like. Thus, as already illustrated under the respective patterns:

Yes/No Question	Statement
^{2}da ^{3}Na̋poli^{3} ↑	^{2}da ^{1}Na̋poli^{1} ↓
^{2}glielo ^{3}da̋^{3} ↑	^{2}glielo ^{1}da̋^{1} ↓
^{3}sı̋^{3} ↑	^{1}sı̋^{1} ↓

The basic intonation for yes/no questions is not normally appropriate for utterances containing a grammatically interrogative word (e.g., chi, cosa, come). So, for example, ^{3}cósa dobbiámo ^{1}fáre^{1} ↓ despite its /. . . ^{1} ˝ ^{1} ↓/ intonation is understood as a question because it contains the interrogative form cosa. An interrogative type of intonation is also much used with interrogative word phrases, as, for example, ^{3}cőme^{3} ↑. This, however, is not an example of the basic /. . . ^{3} ˝ ^{3} ↑/, as we shall shortly see when we discuss a few of the common departures from the basic patterns—departures which speakers use to transmit editorially colored or loaded messages.

6.3. DEPARTURES FROM THE BASIC PATTERNS

Given the Italian intonation system of four pitches, with as many as five pitch points, and three terminal contours, the total number of potentially existing patterns is obviously huge. Although not nearly all the possible variations are current, the number of them which Italians actually use to communicate attitudes and nuances of meaning—all of which are easily and quickly responded to by other speakers of the language—is very considerable. To enumerate and describe them all would be beyond the scope of the present volume. We nonetheless do attempt here to impart a general notion of the kinds of departures in common use. These can be divided into six types: (1) shift of terminal contour, (2) use of the terminal →, (3) shift of pitch level at given pitch points, (4) use of the overhigh pitch, (5) the pre-final pitch point, (6) the displaced center.

1. In questions containing an interrogative word, falling ↓ is often replaced by rising ↑, although the pitch points and levels remain the same. This indicates personal involvement or self-interest on the part of the speaker, and admits to curiosity about the answer. For example:

^{3}cóme si ^{1}chia̋ma^{1} ↓ (basic: no involvement)

^{3}cóme si ^{1}chia̋ma^{1} ↑ (curiosity in relation to speaker's personal experience)

^{2}ma ^{3}cósa vo^{1}le̋vano^{1} ↓ (straight request for information)

^{2}ma ^{3}cósa vo^{1}le̋vano^{1} ↑ (what can they have wanted, with relation to me, or us

2. The terminal →, which does not occur in the basic patterns, is extremely common at the end of non-final phrases—that is, stretches to be followed by more material under another and separate intonation. The meaning is then <u>More coming</u>, and is often crucial when the speaker hesitates. For example:

^{2}número trentas^{3}se̋tte^{3}→ ^{2}intérno ^{1}dűe^{1} ↓

^{2}űno^{2}→ ^{2}dűe^{2}→ ^{2}tre̋^{2}→ ^{1}qua̋ttro^{1} ↓

^{2}sűbito^{2}→ ^{2}si^{1}gnőre^{1} ↓

^{2}nel cinquan^{3}tőtto^{3}→ (pause, but more to come)

Note the contrast, in the last example, with:

^{2}nel cinquan^{3}tőtto^{3} ↑ (interrogation)

Use of → at the end of an utterance also often signals that one speaker would like the other speaker to repeat an earlier utterance from the point marked by the terminal, thus:

^{2}si trattáva ^{3}dí˝^{3}→

It occurs also as the terminal of oft-repeated conventional expressions to indicate routine politeness:

^{1}buon ^{2}giőrno^{2}→ or ^{2}buon ^{3}giőrno^{3}→

^{2}pre̋go^{2}→ or ^{3}pre̋go^{3}→

^{1}per^{2}me̋sso^{2}→

3. Potentially the level at any one of the pitch points of an utterance may be shifted from that of the basic patterns. Very commonly the center of /. . . ^{1} ˝ ^{1}↓/ is raised to high, the result being to narrow the focus on the center for the purpose of emphasizing it or contrasting it with some alternative possibility. For example:

^{3}Léi déve andáre di ^{3}la̋^{1} ↓ (there, not here)

^{2}mi ^{3}chiámo Giu^{3}se̋ppe^{1} ↓ (not Giovanni, or any other name)

Raised centers are so common as to be almost the rule with interrogative words:

^{3}qua̋ndo^{1} ↓

^{2}per^{3}che̋^{1} ↓

with imperative forms of verbs, to add polite solicitousness:

^{2}s'ac^{3}c̋omodi^{1} ↓

^{2}mi ^{3}dí̋ca^{1} ↓

and in exchanges of amenities:

^{3}tánte ^{3}gra̋zie^{1} ↓

^{3}pre̋go^{1} ↓

Expressions of this sort spoken with the basic intonation pattern would risk sounding indifferent, impolite, or even sarcastic.

An interrogative word spoken with an interrogative intonation—for example, ^{3}chí̋^{3} ↑, ^{3}dőve^{3} ↑ — signals something like "How's that again? Please repeat or clarify." In longer utterances of this type, where the interrogative word precedes the center, the pattern is not the basic /^{2} ^{3} ˝ ^{3} ↑/ (cf. ^{2}Léi é venúto ^{3}ie̋ri^{3} ↑), but rather /^{3} ^{3} ˝ ^{3} ↑/, with the interrogative generating a high initial, as in:

^{3}chí é venúto ^{3}ie̋ri^{3} ↑

^{3}dóve si ^{3}sce̋nde^{3} ↑

Unstressed material preceding the interrogative word is on the middle pitch:

^{2}con ^{3}chí an^{3}diámo^{3} ↑

4. The overhigh pitch has a distribution parallel to that of the high in all patterns, and is present in all so-called "exclamations." Any utterance containing it is by definition emotionally colored: it expresses incredulity, surprise, delight, excitement, frustration, anger, scorn, and the like. The nuances conveyed being extremely varied, we give here merely a random list of typical utterances, glossed with interpretations in English:

^{2}ché ^{4}cősa^{2} ↓	What ever was that?
^{2}ma ^{4}ché ^{2}dí̋ci^{2} ↓	I don't believe a word!
^{2}dav^{4}ve̋ro^{4} ↑	Honest and truly?
^{4}ché desídera ^{1}le̋i^{1} ↓	Well, just what do you want?
^{2}Ȅh^{2} → ^{4}cóme ^{2}fa̋i^{2} ↓	Say, just how do you do that?
^{4}acci^{3}de̋nti^{3} →	Damn!
^{2}buon ^{4}giőrno^{1} ↓	Well, so you finally got up!
^{2}mi dis^{4}pia̋ce^{2} ↓	I'm so sorry!

5. For expressing some such attitude of reassurance as "This is obvious; anyone should realize it, but I'm saying it anyway," there exists a pattern distinguished by a pre-final pitch point. This pre-final pitch is normally one level higher than the center and final, which are alike. The terminal is always falling. Examples:

^{3}básta che sáppia il mio ^{1}nő^{2}me^{1} ↓

^{2}ma ^{3}nón vóglio stáre tútta la gior^{1}na̋^{2}ta^{1} ↓

^{4}hó ten^{2}ta̋^{3}to^{2} ↓

^{4}méno ^{2}ma̋^{3}le^{2} ↓

6. Normally the center of intonation is at the last stressed syllable of the phrase, as in all examples cited above. It can, however, be displaced to an earlier stressed syllable, in order to focus constrastive emphasis on the word that contains it. The pitch of a displaced center is normally high or overhigh, as in the following examples:

^{3}próvi un'^{3}a̋ltra péra^{1} ↓

^{2}mi ^{3}páre che non ^{3}vie̋ne staséra^{1} ↓

^{3}ché ^{4}fre̋ddo sta facéndo^{2} ↓

^{4}őggi vánno vía^{4} ↑

The number of situations in which the center of an Italian intonation can be displaced is limited to some grammatical arrangements, and must be considered strictly as a departure from basic patterning. This constitutes one of the major differences between the intonation of Italian and that of English, in which a "movable center" is a feature of basic patterning.

Extended stretches of conversation contain successive intonation patterns standing in fixed sequences. An analysis of the sequences would involve a much more detailed study than space allows. The most that can be done here is to offer an illustration in fragmentary form:

(woman giving directions) ^{3}É lon^{1}ta̋no^{1} → ^{1}Vía della ^{1}Scrőfa^{1} ↓ ^{3}Vía della Scrófa dev'^{1}e̋ssere^{1} → ^{1}per cónto ^{2}mi̋o^{2} ↑ ^{2}nei pa^{3}ra̋ggi di^{3} → ^{3}di^{3} → ^{3}di San ^{1}Pie̋tro^{1} ↓ ^{3}Ah ^{1}e̋cco^{1} ↓ ^{2}Vía della Scrófa é ^{3}dópo l'Argen^{1}ti̋na^{1} ↓ ^{3}dópo il ^{1}Pa̋ntheon^{1} ↓ ^{3}Al^{1}lőra^{1} ↓ ^{3}lí non é nemméno lon^{1}ta̋^{2}no^{1} ↓ ^{2}Vía della ^{3}Scrófa sa^{1}re̋bbe^{1} ↓ ^{3}príma si scende con l'áuto físno all'Argen^{1}ti̋na^{1} ↓ ^{3}pói si tra^{2}vérsa la ^{1}stra̋da^{1} → ^{3}per an^{2}dáre al ^{1}Pa̋ntheon^{1} → ^{4}Quándo ^{2}séi al ^{3}Pa̋ntheon^{3} ↑ ^{2}c'é da do^{3}man^{1}da̋^{2}re^{1} ↓ ^{2}ma ^{3}é vi^{1}cíno^{1} ↓ ^{2}Si svólta una stra^{3}détta stret^{4}ti̋na^{4} ↑ ^{2}e si ^{2}tróva ^{3}súbito^{3} → ^{3}Vía della ^{1}Scrőfa^{1} ↓ ^{3}É faci^{4}li̋ssimo^{2} → ^{2}tróvare Vía della ^{1}Scrőfa^{1} ↓

English

6.4. THE BASIC PATTERNS

Like Italian, English has two basic patterns, both of highly frequent occurrence, for the transmission of uncolored messages. Also as in Italian, one pattern is used in yes/no questions and the other elsewhere. In both, the phrase stress and therefore the center may be in any position relative to the other word stresses of the utterance. Neither pattern has a pre-central or a pre-final pitch point.

1. The pattern used for utterances other than yes/no questions may be stated by the formula /(2) 3 ˝ 1↓/: high center, low final, falling terminal. The parenthesized (2) symbolizes a predictable feature: when syllabic material precedes the center, there is an initial middle pitch. Thus:

/^{3} ˝ ^{1}↓/	^{3}yế̋s^{1} ↓ ^{3}tha̋nk yóu^{1} ↓ ^{3}a̋sk him fór it^{1} ↓
/^{2} ^{3} ˝ ^{1}↓/	^{2}good ^{3}e̋vening^{1} ↓ ^{2}cóme ^{3}thi̋s wáy^{1} ↓ ^{2}the ^{3}tra̋in's cóming^{1} ↓ ^{2}whát ^{3}ti̋me ís it^{1} ↓ ^{2}hów ^{3}a̋re yóu^{1} ↓ ^{2}hów are ^{3}yőu^{1} ↓

2. The pattern used in yes/no questions may be stated by the formula /(2) 3 ˝ 3↑/: center and final both high, terminal rising. The parenthesized (2) has the same value as in the other basic pattern. Thus:

/^{3} ˝ ^{3}↑/	^{3}yế̋s^{3} ↑ ^{3}ha̋s he^{3} ↑ ^{3}őranges^{3} ↑ ^{3}mű́st I dó it^{3} ↑
/^{2} ^{3} ˝ ^{3}↑/	^{2}in ^{3}I̋taly^{3} ↑ ^{2}was thát ^{3}Pa̋ul^{3} ↑ ^{2}is the ^{3}bűs cóming^{3} ↑ ^{2}do you ^{3}knőw them áll^{3} ↑ ^{2}do you knów them ^{3}a̋ll^{3} ↑

Just as they do in Italian, the two basic patterns of English stand in functional contrast in certain minimal pairs, distinguishing yes/no questions from other types of sentence. Thus:

Yes/No Question	Statement
^{2}hére at ^{3}h̋ome^3 ↑	^{2}hére at ^{3}h̋ome^1 ↓
^{2}befóre síx o^{3}cl̋ock^3 ↑	^{2}befóre síx o^{3}cl̋ock^1 ↓

In English, such minimal pairs are almost entirely restricted to verbless phrases; where bal material is present, it is differently arranged, relative to the subject, in questions thar statement—for example:

^{2}háven't they ^{3}fínished^3 ↑: ^{2}they háven't ^{3}fínished^1 ↓

Given such grammatical clues, the contrasting intonations carry a much lower functional than in Italian, where so often they are the only differentiating factor—for example:

^{2}non hánno termi^{3}n̋ato^3 ↑: ^{2}non ^{3}hánno termi^{1}n̋ato^1 ↓

The basic intonation for yes/no questions is not normally appropriate for utter ances which contain a grammatically interrogative word (e.g., who, why, how). Thus, for ample, ^{2}whén was she ^{3}he̋re^1 ↓, despite its /(2) 3 ˝ 1↓/ pattern, is marked as a question be cause it contains the interrogative word when. As in Italian, the interrogative intonation i therefore available with interrogative words to convey additional meaning.

6.5. DEPARTURES FROM THE BASIC PATTERNS

As in Italian, so also in English relatively few of the potentially available arra ments of pitch levels, pitch points, and terminal contours pass currency. Again we treat t more commonly heard variations according to types: (1) shift of terminal contour, (2) use the terminal →, (3) use of basic /(2) 3 ˝ 3↑/ with interrogative words, (4) the overhigh pit (5) the pre-central pitch point, (6) the pre-final pitch point.

1. In questions containing an interrogative word, falling ↓ is often replaced by rising ↑—an indication of personal interest or curiosity on the part of the speaker. In add to shifting the terminal, the basic high center and low final are both drawn to middle, wher material preceding the lowered center rises from middle to high. For example:

^{2}whén was she ^{3}he̋re^1 ↓	(basic: no involvement)
^{3}whén was she ^{2}he̋re^2 ↑	(curiosity in relation to speaker's exper
^{2}so whát did they ^{3}w̋ant^1 ↓	(straight request for information)
^{3}so whát did they ^{2}w̋ant^2 ↑	(what, with relation to me or us)

As we have seen, this shift has its parallel—in meaning as well as in structur in Italian. In English, however, the shifted terminal is frequent in declarations as well, an expresses various kinds of involvement on the part of speaker, or listener, or both. Here shift may be accompanied by a change in all levels as above, or merely by a raising of the final to middle pitch. Examples:

^{2}I dón't ^{3}knőw^{1} ↓	(straight; a bit final)
^{3}I dón't ^{2}knőw^{2} ↑	(indifferent or defensive)
^{2}I dón't ^{3}knőw^{2} ↑	(but I wish I did)
^{2}máybe it ^{3}i̋s^{1} ↓	(straight)
^{3}máybe it ^{2}i̋s^{2} ↑	(I really don't care)
^{2}máybe it ^{3}i̋s^{2} ↑	(though I doubt it)
^{2}the ^{3}ta̋xi's hére^{1} ↓	(fact)
^{2}the ^{3}ta̋xi's here^{2} ↑	(situation affecting you or me or us)

The shift to /(3) 2 ˝ 2↑/ is also common in conventional phrases, where it adds cheeriness or warmth:

^{3}yóu're ^{2}we̋lcome^{2} ↑
^{3}góod ^{2}mőrning^{2} ↑
^{3}I'm ^{2}sőrry^{2} ↑

2. The terminal →, which does not occur in the basic patterns, is commonest at the end of non-final phrases. As in Italian, the meaning is "more coming," and is often crucial when the speaker hesitates. For example:

^{2}are you ^{3}re̋ading^{3} → ^{3}ste̋ve^{3} ↑
^{2}őne^{2} → ^{2}twő^{2} → ^{2}thre̋e^{2} → ^{3}főur^{1} ↓
^{2}sée you ^{3}la̋ter^{2} → ^{2}pe̋te^{2} ↑
^{2}so I ^{3}lőoked at him^{2} →

3. As in Italian, an interrogative word uttered with an interrogative intonation—for example, ^{3}<u>whő</u>^{3} ↑, ^{3}<u>whe̋re</u>^{3} ↑—asks for repetition or further explanation. This is the basic pattern /(2) 3 ˝ 3↑/, used for this special purpose with material normally spoken with the other basic pattern. In longer utterances of this type, the center is usually on the interrogative word, thus:

^{3}whe̋re did you sée it^{3} ↑
^{2}but ^{3}whe̋n was thát^{3} ↑

4. The overhigh pitch, in English as in Italian, has a distribution parallel to that of the high, and bespeaks emotion. Some random examples:

^{2}of ^{4}cőurse we wón't^{1} ↓
^{3}őh^{3} → ^{4}áll ^{2}ri̋ght^{2} ↑

^{2}you méan you gót ^{4}tha̋t fár^{4} ↑
^{2}I dón't thínk I ^{4}li̋ke thát^{3} ↑

5. A pre-central pitch point occurs in occasional utterances as a variation on the basic /(2) 3 ˝ 1↓/. As distinct from the initial middle pitch, the pre-central is high like the center. The effect is to focus on some element that precedes the center, while still not removing the normal emphasis on the center. So:

^{2}the máil tóok ^{3}fi̋fteen ^{3}da̋ys^{1} ↓

Either the pre-central or the center or both may rise to overhigh for different relative emphases.

6. A pre-final pitch point occurs only in the unusual pattern /1 ˝ 3 2↓/, expressing something like perfunctory enthusiasm:

^{1}wőn^{3}derful^{2} ↓
^{1}ce̋r^{3}tainly^{2} ↓

6.6. COMPARISON OF ITALIAN AND ENGLISH

The foregoing analysis of the phonemic intonation patterns and their respectiv distributions in the two languages, though far from complete, reveals at least four proble areas in which native intonation habits may be expected to interfere with an English speaker's efforts at authentic-sounding Italian.

The major problem is perhaps that resulting from the free position of the Eng lish center versus the relatively fixed location of the Italian center at the last stress of the phrase. Since an English speaker says:

^{2}the tráin léaves at ^{3}ni̋ne^{1} ↓
or: ^{2}the tráin ^{3}le̋aves at níne^{1} ↓
or: ^{2}the ^{3}tra̋in léaves at níne^{1} ↓

in accordance with which element of the message he wishes to focus on (nine, not eight or ten; leaves, not arrives; the train, not the plane), he will tend to take the same sort of liberty with the Italian sequence il treno parte alle nove, putting the center of the intonation at nove or at parte or at treno, focusing as he wishes. Italian, however, with its relativel fixed center, handles this sort of contrast by ordering the components of the sentence differently, so that the element under focus comes at the center, in some such way as the following:

^{2}il ^{3}tréno párte alle ^{3}nőve^{1} ↓
or: ^{2}alle ^{3}nóve il tréno ^{3}pa̋rte^{1} ↓
or: ^{2}alle ^{3}nóve párte il ^{3}tre̋no^{1} ↓

As a corollary of his reliance on faulty intonation in this area, the English speaker will of course be slow to learn certain important differences of word order between English and Italian.

For the basic uncolored Italian /. . . 1 ˝ 1↓/ the English speaker will tend to substitute his own basic /(2) 3 ˝ 1↓/, with high center. As a result the Italian may hear something close to his variation /. . . 3 ˝ 1↓/ (see ¶ 6.3), which to him is not uncolored but rather contains an element of emphatic or contrastive insistence. Thus, for example:

expected Italian basic: ^{2}sono arri^{3}váti alle ^{1}ci̋nque^{1} ↓
with English basic substitute: ^{2}sono arriváti alle ^{3}ci̋nque^{1} ↓
will sound closer to the insistent: ^{2}sono arri^{3}váti alle ^{3}ci̋nque^{1} ↓

In both languages, it is common in some instances to shift a basic terminal from falling to rising, but this departure has a wider distribution in English. When the shift occurs in a sentence containing an interrogative word, the English effect on the Italian will not be particularly startling, as, for example, in:

expected Italian: ^{3}cóme si fá per andáre ad ^{1}Ő̋stia^{1} ↑
with English substitute: ^{3}cóme si fá per andáre ad ^{2}Ő̋stia^{2} ↑

When, however, the terminal is shifted in non-interrogative sentences, as the English speaker will often do in order to inject warmth, the effect may be missed and the intonation uninterpretable:

expected Italian: ^{2}mi dis^{3}pia̋ce^{1} ↓
with English substitute: ^{3}mi dis^{2}pia̋ce^{2} ↑

In greetings or the like, the use of terminal → in English is perfunctory or even somewhat cool, as, for example, in

^{2}good ^{3}mőrning^{3} → or just ^{3}mőrning^{3} →

The English speaker will therefore not easily bring himself to use this pattern for the expression of routine but cordial politeness in Italian, as in:

^{2}buon ^{3}giőrno^{3} →

If instead he says something like:

^{2}buon ^{3}giőrno^{1} ↓

the effect on the Italian hearer is likely to be impersonal, distant, or cool.

INDEX